Wisdom in Action

Wisdom in Action

by
John MacArthur, Jr.

MOODY PRESS
CHICAGO

All Scripture quotations in chapters 1-2, unless noted otherwise, are from the *New American Standard Bible,* © 1960, 1962, 1963, 1968, 1971, 1972, 1973, 1975, and 1977 by The Lockman Foundation, and are used by permission.

All Scripture quotations in chapters 3-5, unless noted otherwise, are from the *New Scofield Reference Bible,* King James Version. Copyright © 1967 by Oxford University Press, Inc. Reprinted by permission.

Library of Congress Cataloging in Publication Data

MacArthur, John, 1939-
    Wisdom in action / by John MacArthur, Jr.
       p.   cm.   (John MacArthur's Bible studies)
    Originally delivered at Grace Community Church, Panorama City, Calif.
    Includes indexes.
    ISBN O-8024-5359-7
    1. Bible. N.T. James III, 13-18—Criticism, interpretation, etc.
    2. Bible. N.T. Ephesians V, 15-17—Criticism, interpretation, etc.
    3. Wisdom—Biblical teaching. I. Title. II. Series: MacArthur, John, 1939-   Bible studies.
    BS2785.2.M244   1988
    227'.9106—dc19   88-838
                                            CIP

1 2 3 4 5 6 7 8 Printing/LC/Year 93 92 91 90 89 88

Printed in the United States of America

Contents

These Bible studies are taken from messages delivered by Pastor-Teacher John MacArthur, Jr., at Grace Community Church in Panorama City, California. The recorded messages themselves may be purchased as a series or individually. Please request the current price list by writing to:

WORD OF GRACE COMMUNICATIONS
P.O. Box 4000
Panorama City, CA 91412

Or call the following toll-free number:
1-800-55-GRACE

1
Earthly and Heavenly Wisdom—Part 1

Outline

Introduction
A. The Proof of Wisdom
B. The Pursuit of Wisdom
   1. The establishment of Solomon's wisdom
     a) His lack of understanding
     b) His need for understanding
   2. The extent of Solomon's wisdom
   3. The essence of Solomon's wisdom
C. The Possession of Wisdom
D. The Premium of Wisdom

Lesson
I. The Manifestation of Wisdom (v. 13)
   A. The Claim
   B. The Questions
     1. Who is really understanding?
     2. Who is really wise?
   C. The Command
   D. The Proof
     1. Our good behavior
     2. Our good deeds
     3. Our meekness
       a) Displayed
       b) Defined
         (1) As a character trait
         (2) As power under control

A Bible Study on Wisdom

Introduction

James 3:13-18 is a comparison between wisdom from above, which is pure, peaceable, gentle, reasonable, full of mercy and good fruits, unwavering, and without hypocrisy (v. 17), and wisdom from below, which is earthly, natural, and demonic (v. 15). James affirms what the Old Testament wisdom literature taught—that wisdom is divided into two realms: the wisdom of man and the wisdom of God.

A. The Proof of Wisdom

Men claim to possess wisdom. But is it the wisdom of men or the wisdom of God? There's a great difference. James 3:13 says, "Who among you is wise and understanding?

8

Let him show by his good behavior his deeds in the gentleness of wisdom." If you claim to have wisdom from above, the burden of proof lies with you.

B. The Pursuit of Wisdom

According to philosophers throughout the ages, man should strive to acquire wisdom. Roman orator Cicero, of the first century B.C., said that wisdom is the best gift of the gods—the mother of all good things—the best and that which generates the best. Most philosophers throughout history have believed that if a person could acquire anything, it should be wisdom, because wisdom would allow him to obtain anything else. That philosophy matches Scripture. Proverbs 4:7 says, "Acquire wisdom; and with all your acquiring, get understanding."

1. The establishment of Solomon's wisdom

   a) His lack of understanding

   First Kings 3:5 tells us that "in Gibeon the Lord appeared to Solomon in a dream at night; and God said, 'Ask what you wish me to give you.'" Wouldn't it be wonderful for God to say that to you? Solomon replied, "Thou hast shown great lovingkindness to Thy servant David my father, according as he walked before Thee in truth and righteousness and uprightness of heart toward Thee; and Thou hast reserved for him this great lovingkindness, that Thou hast given him a son to sit on his throne, as it is this day. And now, O Lord my God, Thou hast made thy servant king in place of my father David, yet I am but a little child; I do not know how to go out or come in. And Thy servant is in the midst of Thy people which Thou hast chosen, a great people who cannot be numbered or counted for multitude" (vv. 6-8).

   b) His need for understanding

   Solomon had all the possessions, honor, rank, and power a person could want. So this is what he asked for: "Give thy servant an understanding heart to judge Thy people to discern between good and evil. For who is able to judge this great people of Thine?" (v. 9). Verses 10-14 say, "It was pleasing in the sight of the Lord that Solomon had asked this thing. And God said to him, 'Because you have asked this thing and have not asked for yourself long life, nor have asked riches for yourself, nor have you asked for the life of your enemies, but have asked for yourself discernment to understand justice, behold, I have done according to your words. Behold, I have given you a wise and discerning heart, so that there has been no one like you before you, nor shall one like you arise after you. And I have also given you what you have not asked, both riches and honor, so that there will not be any among the kings like you all your days. And if you walk in my ways, keeping my statutes and commandments, as your father David walked, then I will prolong your days.' " Solomon asked for wisdom, and it was wonderfully bestowed on him.

2. The extent of Solomon's wisdom

First Kings 4:29-34 reveals the extent of the wisdom God gave Solomon: "Now God gave Solomon wisdom and very great discernment and breadth of mind, like the sand that is on the seashore. And Solomon's wisdom surpassed the wisdom of all the sons of the east and all the wisdom of Egypt. For he was wiser than all men, than Ethan the Ezrahite, Heman, Calcol and Darda, the sons of Mahol; and his fame was known in all the surrounding nations. He also spoke 3,000 proverbs, and his songs were 1,005. And he spoke of trees, from the cedar that is in Lebanon even to the hyssop that grows on the wall; he spoke also of animals and birds and creeping things and fish. And men came from all peoples to hear the wisdom of Solomon, from all the kings of the earth who had heard of his wisdom."

3. The essence of Solomon's wisdom

First Kings 5:12 says, "The Lord gave wisdom to Solomon, just as He promised Him." Haven't those who know anything about the Bible extolled the wisdom of Solomon and affirmed that the greatest thing a man could have is wisdom? The wisdom Solomon received was predominantly human wisdom—a wisdom that relates to the created world. Solomon needed such wisdom to render justice in the nation he ruled over. But certainly God made available to him His wisdom—a wisdom far deeper than mere human wisdom.

C. The Possession of Wisdom

In Deuteronomy 32:29 Moses cries out in pain over the apostasy of Israel, saying, "Would that they were wise . . . !" He had in mind spiritual wisdom. In the midst of an inexplicable series of events, Job sought such wisdom from God (e.g., Job 28:12). He understood that wisdom was the highest, most noble, and most valuable of all possessions.

In Psalm 2:10 the psalmist calls for the kings of the earth to be wise. Ezra 7:25 tells us God gave Ezra wisdom to lead the nation Israel, which had been brought out of captivity in Babylon. Daniel 1:17 tells us God granted Daniel and his friends knowledge and skill in all branches of learning and wisdom. The king of Babylon himself affirmed that Daniel possessed excellent wisdom (Dan. 5:14). The apostle Paul prayed that every believer might be given "a spirit of wisdom and of revelation in the knowledge of [Christ]" (Eph. 1:17).

D. The Premium of Wisdom

Whether wisdom is approached from a philosophical perspective or a scriptural one, man sets a premium on wisdom. For example, as one raises his children, he trains them to be wise. Living well requires more than knowledge; it requires wisdom. You need to know how to apply what you know in every situation. God calls all men to be wise. Matthew 10:16 says to "be shrewd as serpents, and innocent as doves."

Lesson

I. THE MANIFESTATION OF WISDOM (v. 13)

"Who among you is wise and understanding? Let him show by his good behavior his deeds in the gentleness of wisdom."

From James's perspective, wisdom is made manifest by the way a person conducts his life. How you live illustrates whether you possess true wisdom.

James began the third chapter of his epistle by saying, "Let not many of you become teachers" (v. 1). Some scholars believe the entire chapter deals only with teachers, but I believe that once he introduced the subject of teachers, he moved to a discussion of the tongue and how it relates to everyone, not just teachers. When James begins his discussion of wisdom, he's no longer dealing with teachers of God's Word, but everyone. Any person's wisdom is manifest by how he lives his life, just as any person's speech tends to reveal what's in his heart.

A. The Claim

Many people claim to be wise. No fool in our world is a self-confessed fool—everyone believes he's an expert. We live in a sea of opinions. Frankly, no one's opinion is worth more than anyone else's. When people want to give an expert opinion, however, they often will quote a psychologist or a psychiatrist, unless it is in regard to a fact that demands a scientific, categorical answer.

B. The Questions

1. Who is really understanding?

The Greek word translated "understanding" is used only here in the New Testament. It refers to a specialist or a professional highly skilled in applying his knowledge to practical situations.

2. Who is really wise?

The Greek word translated "wise" is *sophos*. The Greeks used it to refer to speculative knowledge, theory, and philosophy. But the Hebrews infused wisdom with a deeper meaning: skillfully applying knowledge to the matter of practical living.

James was asking, "Who among you has practical skill? Who among you is truly a professional and specialist in the art of living?"

C. The Command

Anyone who possesses knowledge, understanding, skill, and wisdom will show it in his life. Divine wisdom in the heart of a person produces a changed life. That's why James says, "Let him show by his good behavior his deeds" (v. 13). The phrase translated "let him show" is an aorist imperative in the Greek text. It is a command to demonstrate one's wisdom and understanding. That is the thrust of James 2:14-26, summarized in verse 26: "Faith without works is dead." A person's claim to have faith will be validated by his works. Verse 18 says, "Someone may well say, 'You have faith, and I have works; show me your faith without the works, and I will show you my faith by my works.' " Similarly, James is saying that if you claim to be wise, you need to demonstrate it.

D. The Proof

How can we show that we possess the wisdom of God— the God-given ability to understand ourselves, our world, and God's truth?

1. Our good behavior

In James 3:13 James says one of the ways we prove that we possess God's wisdom is through our "good behavior." That is a general statement referring to good conduct. We could translate the Greek word *anastrophēs* as "life-style" or "activity." The Greek word translated "good" means "lovely," "beautiful," "attractive," "noble," or "excellent." Anyone who claims to have divine wisdom and living faith will show it by his good behavior and excellent life-style.

2. Our good deeds

Then James becomes specific when he says, "Let him show by his good behavior his deeds." He is focusing on the details. The wisdom of God alters not only your general conduct but also what you do specifically. Every act within a person's life is consistent with how he conducts his entire life. If it is a life based on the wisdom of God, each aspect of his life will reveal that.

3. Our meekness

a) Displayed

A believer will demonstrate that he possesses the wisdom of God not only in what he does generally or specifically but also in his attitude. In verse 13 James says, "Let him show by his good behavior his deeds in the gentleness of wisdom." True wisdom is characterized by meekness. Most people I have met who believe they're wise are actually arrogant. A person who possesses the wisdom of God is far from arrogant; he is meek. In verse 14 James says, "If you have bitter jealousy and selfish ambition in your heart, do not be arrogant and so lie against the truth." James knew well the angry, arrogant, divisive spirit often demonstrated by professing Christians who believe they're wise. Such an attitude reveals the absence of meekness, a characteristic of God's wisdom.

b) Defined

(1) As a character trait

The word translated "gentleness" is *prautēs* (Gk., *praus*, "gentle" or "meek"). It is the opposite of self-promotion and arrogance. It is a trait that characterized the Lord. In Matthew 11:29 He says, "Take my yoke upon you, and learn of me; for I

14

am meek and lowly in heart" (KJV*). It is also a trait belonging to all the members of His kingdom. In Matthew 5:5 the Lord says, "Blessed are the meek; for they shall inherit the earth" (KJV). James 1:21 says to put "aside all filthiness and all that remains of wickedness, [and] in humility receive the word implanted." Meekness also is a fruit of the Spirit (Gal. 5:23).

(2) As power under control

Praus is often used of a gentle voice, a gentle breeze, or a gentle animal. In reference to people it means "gracious" or "mild." We might translate it as "tender." It was used of a horse that was broken. The Greeks characterized meekness as power under control. It is a freedom from malice, bitterness, or any desire for revenge. Commentator William Barclay said meekness according to Greek thought is not a spineless gentleness, a sentimental fondness, or a passive quietism but strength under control (*The Gospel of Matthew*, vol. 1 [Philadelphia: Westminster, 1958], pp. 91-93). Numbers 12:3 tells us Moses was the meekest man on the earth, yet he could act decisively with righteous anger when the occasion arose. And where true meekness exists, such anger will not be self-seeking; it will defend God's righteousness. To be meek is to be under control, which in the believer's case means to be under the control of God.

The only way to truly define meekness is in the context of relationships because it refers to how we treat others. It should characterize our relationship with man and God.

James was saying a man proves the divine source of his wisdom by his life. The general pattern of his life and the specific things he does will reflect the work, the way, and the will of God, and his attitude will be one of humility, gentleness, mildness, and meekness.

*King James Version.

15

The Attitude of the Truly Wise

In his wonderful commentary on the book of James, Robert Johnstone wrote the following about meekness: "I do not know that at any point the opposition between the spirit of the world and the spirit of Christ is more marked, more obviously diametrical, than with regard to this feature of character. That 'the meek' should 'inherit the earth'—they that bear wrongs, and exemplify the love which 'seeketh not her own'—to a world that believes in high-handedness and self-assertion, and pushing the weakest to the wall, a statement like this of the Lord from heaven cannot but appear an utter paradox. The man of the world desires to be counted anything but 'meek' or 'poor in spirit,' and would deem such a description of him equivalent to a charge of unmanliness. Ah, brethren, this is because we have taken in Satan's conception of manliness instead of God's. One man has been shown us by God, in whom His ideal of man was embodied; and He, when He was reviled, reviled not again; when He suffered, threatened not, but committed Himself to Him that judgeth righteously: He for those who nailed Him to the tree prayed, 'Father, forgive them; for they know not what they do.' The world's spirit of wrath, then, must be folly; whilst than a spirit of meekness like His, in the midst of controversy, oppositions, trials of whatever kind, there can be no surer evidence that 'Jesus is made of God to His people wisdom' " (*The Epistle of James* [Minneapolis: Klock & Klock, 1978 reprint], pp. 272-73). Johnstone recognized more than a hundred years ago what we recognize today—that the wisdom of man is arrogant, conceited, and self-serving, whereas the wisdom of God is humble, meek, and non-retaliatory.

Johnstone further says, "We have here again what may be described as the central thought of this Epistle, that where religion has real saving hold of a mind and heart, it cannot from its nature but powerfully influence the outward life; and that the more a Christian has of true wisdom and spiritual knowledge, the more manifestly will his life at all points be governed by his religion. Talk of orthodoxy and Christian experience, however fluent and animated and clever, does not of itself prove wisdom; the really wise man will 'show his works' " (p. 271). Many people in the church claim to possess the wisdom of God, but the proof is in the living. The contrast between false wisdom and true wisdom is crystal clear.

Where did James get his information from regarding God's wisdom? What foundation was he working from? James 1:1 tells us he was a Jew writing to other Jews. So he was building his teaching on the Jewish understanding of wisdom from the Old Testament. To understand the difference between the wisdom of God and the wisdom of men, we need only go back to the Old Testament wisdom literature, which consists of Job, Psalms, Proverbs, Ecclesiastes, and the Song of Solomon. Each book is filled with calls to wisdom.

I. THE PERSPECTIVE OF HUMAN WISDOM

A. The Purpose of Ecclesiastes

The book of Ecclesiastes is greatly misunderstood. It is a difficult book to read simply because it is hard to understand. Everything in it appears wrong and as if it doesn't fit with the rest of Scripture. But it is part of the wisdom literature because it is a statement of human wisdom. Ecclesiastes tells us how man perceives his world, God, and the facts of life.

B. The Author of Ecclesiastes

Most scholars believe Ecclesiastes was penned by Solomon. They debate whether he wrote it before he was a true believer or after. He may have written it in retrospect, or he may have penned it sometime before he had a full understanding of the truth of God that changed his life.

C. The Revelation of Ecclesiastes

Ecclesiastes is a fascinating book because it reveals the folly, uselessness, senselessness, and frustration of human wisdom—that which James calls earthly, natural, and demonic (James 3:15).

1. Solomon's abundance of human wisdom

In Ecclesiastes 1:16 Solomon says to himself, "Behold, I have magnified and increased wisdom more than all who were over Jerusalem before me." That verse shows me that when God initially gave Solomon wisdom, He gave it to him on a human level. He gave Solomon wisdom to make successful decisions and judgments as king. But although divine wisdom was available to him, I believe Solomon opted for human wisdom the greater portion of his life. And that wisdom was never able to answer his ultimate questions. Then Solomon said, "My mind has observed a wealth of wisdom and knowledge" (v. 16). Solomon was the wisest man who ever lived. He not only knew wisdom, but he could understand, organize, and apply it.

2. Solomon's attempts to understand human wisdom

   a) He studied folly

   In verse 17 he says, "I set my mind to know wisdom and to know madness [extravagance] and folly." To better understand wisdom Solomon decided to study its opposite. By observing what is foolish you often can gain a greater appreciation for what is wise.

   But Solomon concluded, "I realized that this also is striving after wind" (v. 17). His attempt to enhance the value of human wisdom by studying folly resulted in an effort likened to chasing air. In verse 18 he says, "Because in much wisdom there is much grief, and increasing knowledge results in increasing pain." People say, "Ignorance is bliss. What you don't know can't hurt you." That's not always true, but it is true that the more you know the more responsibility you carry. When Solomon set out to know everything, he experienced the grief and pain inherent in human wisdom.

   b) He tried pleasure

   In Ecclesiastes 2:1 Solomon continues, "I said to myself, Come now, I will test you with pleasure. So enjoy yourself." He was trying to find meaning in life somewhere. He didn't find it in wisdom or folly, so now he was trying pleasure. He indulged himself in every conceivable way. He indulged himself with women, with incredible wealth, with extravagant living, and with great possessions.

His conclusion: "Behold, it too was futility" (v. 1). He couldn't find the meaning of life in pleasure, folly, madness, or wisdom. Look at our world and you'll see the same effort. People seek education. They read, they study, and they learn, but it's futile. The madness in the world can be characterized by those who take drugs or drink alcohol. Then there are people in this world who live for pleasure and possessions. They want a bigger house, a bigger car, better clothes, a bigger diamond. But none of those things come anywhere near to ultimate reality.

c) He tried happiness

In verse 2 Solomon continues, "I said of laughter, 'It is madness,' and of pleasure, 'What does it accomplish?' "

d) He tried wine

Verse 3 says, "I explored with my mind how to stimulate my body with wine while my mind was guiding me wisely, and how to take hold of folly, until I could see what good there is for the sons of men to do under heaven the few years of their lives."

e) He tried building an empire

Verse 4 says, "I enlarged my works: I built houses for myself, I planted vineyards for myself." That is characteristic of a man who believed success in life would come through his power.

f) He tried nature

Then Solomon said, "I made gardens and parks for myself, and I planted in them all kinds of fruit trees; I made ponds of water for myself from which to irrigate a forest of growing trees" (vv. 5-6). Notice he did all those things for himself. That is typical of human wisdom—it is in a mad pursuit to fulfill itself.

19

g) He tried authority

Then Solomon said, "I bought male and female slaves, and I had homeborn slaves. Also I possessed flocks and herds larger than all who preceded me in Jerusalem" (v. 7).

h) He tried collecting

In verse 8 he says, "I collected for myself silver and gold, and the treasure of kings and provinces." He collected fancy artifacts and assembled a museum. Today people pay large sums of money just to collect certain items.

i) He tried music

Then he said, "I provided for myself male and female singers" (v. 8).

j) He tried sex

Solomon also tried "the pleasures of men—many concubines" (v. 8).

k) He tried greatness

Solomon then said, "I became great and increased more than all who preceded me in Jerusalem. My wisdom also stood by me. And all that my eyes desired I did not refuse them. . . . for my heart was pleased because of all my labor and this was my reward for all my labor" (vv. 9-10). Solomon justified every conceivable indulgence.

3. Solomon's attitude toward human wisdom

In verse 11 he says, "Thus I considered all my activities which my hands had done and the labor which I had exerted, and behold all was vanity and striving after wind and there was no profit under the sun." What a tragic conclusion to come to after all that effort!

a) Its weariness

Then Solomon said, "So I hated life" (v. 17). He had all life could give him. He had wine, women, and song. He built an empire. He lived a life of pleasure. He had more than anyone else, yet he hated life, concluding, "Everything is futility and striving after wind" (v. 17).

b) Its selfishness

Verse 18 says, "Thus I hated all the fruit of my labor for which I had labored under the sun." He hated the gold, the silver, the animals, the plants, and the women. Why? Because he found that none of it brought him satisfaction, so he began to resent it all. Then he said, "I must leave it to the man who will come after me" (v. 18). Solomon realized he would die, and someone else would receive what he worked for.

c) Its despair

In verse 20 he says, "I completely despaired of all the fruit of my labor for which I had labored under the sun."

d) Its hopelessness

Verse 21 says, "When there is a man who has labored with wisdom, knowledge and skill, then he gives his legacy to one who has not labored with them. This too is vanity and a great evil."

e) Its grief

In verses 23-24 he says, "Because all his days his task is painful and grievous; even at night his mind does not rest. This too is vanity. There is nothing better for a man than to eat and drink and tell himself that his labor is good." Solomon knew God was the answer to his questions about life, but apparently he wasn't reaching out to God to receive those answers.

4. Solomon's analysis of human wisdom

In Ecclesiastes 8:16-17 Solomon says, "When I gave my heart to know wisdom and to see the task which has been done on the earth (even though one should never sleep day or night), and I saw every work of God, I concluded that man cannot discover the work which has been done under the sun. Even though man should seek laboriously, he will not discover; and though the wise man should say, 'I know,' he cannot discover." Solomon was saying he knew God was at work, but as hard as man might try, he can't discover the reality of godly wisdom. You can't pursue God from the human perspective. That is the dilemma of man today—he believes he is wise but in reality he is a fool. Everything he pursues is useless.

The sum of Solomon's perspective on human wisdom is in Ecclesiastes 4:2-3: "So I congratulated the dead who are already dead more than the living who are still living. But better off than both of them is the one who has never existed." That's a death wish and is the logical end of worldly wisdom. It is earthly, sensual, and demonic. It ends in futility. Isaiah 5:21 says, "Woe to those who are wise in their own eyes." As it is used here, "woe" implies the curse of God. He curses those who depend entirely on worldly wisdom.

The Old Testament gives a dramatic portrayal of earthly, human wisdom. That is what James is building on. When you see an indulgent person trying to get all he can for himself, he obviously does not have the wisdom of God. When you see a person characterized by righteous deeds, holy acts, and a spirit of gentleness, kindness, meekness, and humility, you know he possesses God's wisdom.

II. THE PERSPECTIVE OF GODLY WISDOM

Job, Psalms, and Proverbs tell us about the true wisdom of God and how it differs from worldly wisdom. It has nothing to do with money, sexual fulfillment, building an empire, or amassing a fortune. What then is true wisdom? What can satisfy the heart of man and make life worth living? The wisdom of God alone. As we look at verses in Job, Psalms, and Proverbs, we will discover that God's wisdom is important in developing both a person's behavior and his relationship to God. True wisdom leads to a selfless, humble approach to serving God.

A. The Source of Godly Wisdom

1. Emphasized in the Old Testament

Many texts in the Old Testament tell us that God is the source of true wisdom.

a) Job 9:4—Job observed that God is "wise in heart and mighty in strength." It is God's nature to possess infinite wisdom.

b) Psalm 104:24—The psalmist said, "O Lord, how many are Thy works! In wisdom Thou hast made them all."

c) Proverbs 3:19-20—Solomon wrote, "The Lord by wisdom founded the earth; by understanding He established the heavens. By His knowledge the deeps were broken up, and the skies drip with dew."

God is the source of wisdom. Other texts in addition to the wisdom literature emphasize that fact (Jer. 10:7, 12; Dan. 1:17; 2:20-23).

2. Emphasized in the New Testament

a) Romans 11:33—"Oh, the depth of the riches both of the wisdom and knowledge of God! How unsearchable are His judgments and unfathomable His ways!"

b) Ephesians 3:10—The Lord has accomplished what he has in the church "in order that the manifold wisdom of God might now be made known." God's wisdom is on display in the church.

c) 1 Timothy 1:17—"Now to the King eternal, immortal, invisible, the only God, be honor and glory forever and ever. Amen." Some sources say the "only wise God." He is the God of great and profound wisdom.

d) James 1:5—"If any of you lacks wisdom, let him ask of God, who gives to all men generously and without reproach."

True wisdom comes from God. It is the kind of wisdom that makes life meaningful. It is "first pure, then peaceable, gentle, reasonable, full of mercy and good fruits, unwavering, without hypocrisy" (James 3:17).

B. The Pursuit of Godly Wisdom

Although wisdom comes from God, it is to be pursued by man.

1. The call to wisdom

Job 28 is a call to pursue wisdom.

a) The search for riches

Verses 1-2 say, "Surely there is a mine for silver, and a place where they refine gold. Iron is taken from the dust, and from rock copper is smelted." Job then describes the mining process: "Man puts an end to darkness" (v. 3). Man digs deep into the earth where there is only darkness. He puts an end to that darkness by lighting his candles and lamps to see as he mines the earth. Job continues, "To the farthest limit he searches out the rock in gloom and deep shadow. He sinks a shaft far from habitation, forgotten by the foot; they hang and swing to and fro far from men" (vv. 3-4). In ancient days men would drill a shaft deep into a mountain or the ground, suspend themselves with a rope, and hang in the shaft while they tried to find some metal or precious stone to mine. They exerted great effort.

Verse 5 says, "The earth, from it comes food, and underneath it is turned up as fire." The ancients may have had some way to set fire to the interior of the earth, or explode a certain portion of earth to open up new mining areas. Job continues, "Its rocks are the source of sapphires, and its dust contains gold. The path no bird of prey knows, nor has the falcon's eye

24

caught sight of it. The proud beasts have not trodden it, nor has the fierce lion passed over it. He puts his hand on the flint; he overturns the mountains at the base" (vv. 6-9). Again we get the idea they may have had the means to overturn the foundations of the mountains. Verse 10 says, "He hews out channels through the rocks." We tend to underestimate the people and skills of ancient times, assuming that modern man invented mining. But we must remember that man is in a degenerative process—he's not getting better; he's getting worse. Then Job says, "His eye sees anything precious. He dams up the streams from flowing; and what is hidden he brings out to the light" (vv. 10-11).

b) The search for wisdom

Verse 12 says, "But where can wisdom be found? And where is the place of understanding?" Job is saying that man goes to great efforts to find precious metals, but he can't find wisdom. Here he is articulating the frustration of the preacher in Ecclesiastes. Then Job says, "Man does not know its value, nor is it found in the land of the living. The deep says, 'It is not in me'; and the sea says, 'It is not with me.' Pure gold cannot be given in exchange for it, nor can silver be weighed as its price. It cannot be valued in the gold of Ophir, in precious onyx or sapphire. Gold or glass cannot equal it, nor can it be exchanged for articles of fine gold. Coral and crystal are not to be mentioned; and the acquisition of wisdom is above that of pearls" (vv. 13-18). There's nothing in the world that can buy wisdom, and it can't be found in the things of the world.

Job says, "Where then does wisdom come from? And where is the place of understanding? Thus it is hidden from the eyes of all living, and concealed from the birds of the sky. Abaddon and Death say, 'With our ears we have heard a report of it.' God understands its way; and He knows its place" (vv. 20-23). If you want true wisdom, you go to God. If only the church would believe that, it could clean out a lot of the human philosophy that has encumbered it. God knows where wisdom is because "He looks to the ends of the earth, and sees everything under the heavens. When He imparted weight to the wind, and meted out the waters by measure, when He set a limit for the rain, and a course for the thunderbolt, then He saw it and declared it; He established it and also searched it out. And to man He said, Behold, the fear of the Lord, that is wisdom; and to depart from evil is understanding" (vv. 24-28).

What is true wisdom? To fear God and depart from evil. Wisdom isn't a question of how much you know; it's a matter of whether you love the Lord your God and depart from sin. Men pursue wisdom, but they can't find it because it belongs to God. Only when men pursue God will they know wisdom.

2. The availability of wisdom

   a) Proverbs 1:5—"A wise man will hear and increase in learning, and a man of understanding will acquire wise counsel."

   b) Proverbs 1:20-29—Wisdom is everywhere. In these verses the wisdom of God is personified as a preacher: "Wisdom shouts in the street" (v. 20). Wisdom is available through the voices of the Old and New Testament preachers and anyone who teaches God's Word. Wisdom shouts in the street—it's not hidden or buried in the depths of the earth; it's right there.

   Solomon, the author of most of Proverbs, continues, "She lifts her voice in the square; at the head of the noisy streets she cries out; at the entrance of the gates in the city, she utters her sayings" (vv. 20-21). True wisdom is available. Men simply are looking in the wrong place. Wisdom cries, "How long, O naive ones, will you love simplicity?" (v. 22). The Hebrew word translated "naive" is derived from a root word that means "an open door." Naive people have a mind that's an open door—ideas fly in and out. They are completely undiscerning. Solomon observes that "scoffers delight themselves in scoffing, and fools hate knowledge" (v. 22).

In verses 23-25 wisdom says, "I will pour out my spirit on you; I will make my words known to you, because I called, and you refused; I stretched out my hand, and no one paid attention; and you neglected all my counsel, and did not want my reproof." Who personified wisdom more than anyone else? Jesus Christ. He cried out to the people in the streets, and they responded to Him exactly as verses 23-25 indicate.

Wisdom concludes, "I will even laugh at your calamity; I will mock when your dread comes, when your dread comes like a storm, and your calamity comes on like a whirlwind, when distress and anguish come on you. Then they will call on me, but I will not answer; they will seek me diligently, but they shall not find me, because they hated knowledge, and did not choose the fear of the Lord" (vv. 26-29). True wisdom is to fear God—to hold Him in reverential awe, to love Him, and to turn from iniquity.

c) Proverbs 2:1-7—"My son, if you will receive my sayings, and treasure my commandments within you, make your ear attentive to wisdom, incline your heart to understanding; for if you cry for discernment, lift your voice for understanding; if you seek her as silver, and search for her as for hidden treasures; then you will discern the fear of the Lord, and discover the knowledge of God. For the Lord gives wisdom; from His mouth come knowledge and understanding. He stores up sound wisdom for the upright." The avenue to true wisdom is to fear the Lord and turn from iniquity. Everyone should follow that path.

d) Proverbs 3:13-21—"How blessed is the man who finds wisdom, and the man who gains understanding. For its profit is better than the profit of silver, and its gain than fine gold. She is more precious than jewels; and nothing you desire compares with her. Long life is in her right hand; in her left hand are riches and honor. Her ways are pleasant ways, and all her paths are peace. She is a tree of life to those who take hold of her, and happy are all who hold her fast.

The Lord by wisdom founded the earth; by understanding He established the heavens. By His knowledge the deeps were broken up, and the skies drip with dew. My son, let them not depart from your sight; keep sound wisdom and discretion."

e) Proverbs 4:5, 7-9—"Acquire wisdom! Acquire understanding! Do not forget, nor turn away from the words of my mouth. . . . The beginning of wisdom is: Acquire wisdom; and with all your acquiring, get understanding. Prize her, and she will exalt you; she will honor you if you embrace her. She will place on your head a garland of grace; she will present you with a crown of beauty." Pursue the fear of the Lord and an upright life, and you will know true wisdom and true blessing.

f) Proverbs 7:2-5—"Keep my commandments and live, and my teaching as the apple of your eye. Bind them on your fingers; write them on the tablet of your heart. Say to wisdom, You are my sister, and call understanding your intimate friend; that they may keep you from an adulteress, from the foreigner who flatters with her words."

g) Proverbs 8:1-6, 10-13, 17-21—"Does not wisdom call, and understanding lift up her voice? On top of the heights beside the way, where the paths meet, she takes her stand; beside the gates, at the opening to the city, at the entrance of the doors, she cries out: To you, O men, I call, and my voice is to the sons of men. O naive ones, discern prudence; and, O fools, discern wisdom. Listen, for I shall speak noble things; and the opening of my lips will produce right things. . . . Take my instruction, and not silver, and knowledge rather than choicest gold. For wisdom is better than jewels; and all desirable things can not compare with her. I, wisdom, dwell with prudence, and I find knowledge and discretion. The fear of the Lord is to hate evil; pride and arrogance and the evil way. . . . I love those who love me; and those who diligently seek me will find me. Riches and honor are with me, enduring wealth and righteousness. My fruit is better than gold, even pure gold, and my yield than choicest silver. I walk in the way of righteousness, in the midst of the paths of justice, to endow those who love me with wealth, that I may fill their treasuries."

h) Proverbs 9:6—"Forsake your folly and live."

i) Proverbs 16:16—"How much better is it to get wisdom than gold! And to get understanding is to be chosen above silver."

You can follow the route of man's wisdom, which is earthly, sensual, and demonic. Those who pursue the wisdom of God will fear Him, love Him, seek to do righteousness, and turn from iniquity. God's wisdom brings greater riches than all the riches of the world. Hosea 6:3 says, "So let us know, let us press on to know the Lord." Proverbs 4:13 says, "Take hold of instruction; do not let go. Guard her, for she is your life."

Do you have the wisdom of God? He offers it to you. First Corinthians 1:30 says Christ "became to us the wisdom from God." When you receive Jesus Christ, you receive the wisdom of God—the wisdom that fears God, hates evil, and brings all spiritual blessings. It far surpasses anything the world could offer.

Focusing on the Facts

1. What are the two realms of wisdom (see p. 8)?
2. How does a person prove which kind of wisdom he possesses (see pp. 8-9)?
3. What have philosophers taught about wisdom through the ages? What Scripture verse does that philosophy match (see p. 9)?
4. Why did Solomon ask God to give him wisdom (1 Kings 3:9)? What did God give Solomon in addition to wisdom (1 Kings 3:13; see p. 10)?
5. What was the extent of the wisdom God gave Solomon (1 Kings 4:29-34; see p. 10)?
6. What kind of wisdom did Solomon predominantly use (see p. 11)?

7. Why does living well require more than knowledge (see p. 11)?
8. Define "wise" and "understanding" as used in James 3:13 (see pp. 12-13).
9. What does James command the believer to do in James 3:13 (see p. 13)?
10. In what three ways does a believer prove he possesses the wisdom of God? Explain each one (James 3:13; see pp. 13-14).
11. How did the Greeks characterize meekness? Explain (see p. 15).
12. What foundation is James building his teaching from in James 3:13-18 (see p. 17)?
13. Who wrote Ecclesiastes? Why does it belong with the Old Testament wisdom literature (see p. 17)?
14. Why did Solomon study folly? What was his conclusion (Eccles. 1:17-18; see p. 18)?
15. What things did Solomon try in an effort to understand wisdom (see pp. 18-20)?
16. Worldly wisdom results in what (Eccles. 2:17-24; see p. 21)?
17. What did Solomon conclude about his efforts to understand wisdom (Eccles. 8:16-17; see p. 22)?
18. What is the source of wisdom (see p. 23)?
19. How does Job characterize man's search for riches (Job 28:1-11; see pp. 24-25)?
20. How does Job answer his question in Job 28:12: "Where can wisdom be found" (see pp. 25-26)?
21. Cite some Proverbs that describe the availability of wisdom (see pp. 26-29).
22. What does a person receive additionally when he receives Jesus Christ (see p. 29)?

Pondering the Principles

1. In James 3:13 James commands every believer to prove his possession of God's wisdom in three ways: by his overall behavior, his good deeds, and his meekness. What does your behavior reveal about your wisdom? Do you sometimes display behavior that would lead people to conclude you are dependent on worldly wisdom? Give some examples. What do your specific deeds prove about your wisdom? List some deeds that exemplify God's wisdom and those that reflect worldly wisdom. How about your attitude? Is it characterized by meekness, or do you tend to display an arrogant, selfish attitude towards others? If you have

found it is easier to give examples of behavior and deeds that reflect a worldly wisdom, you may need to re-examine your commitment to God's truth. Pursue the wisdom that God has made available to you.

2. Review the section on Solomon's effort to understand wisdom (see pp. 18-20). He tried many different approaches. Which ones have you tried in the past, and which ones are you dabbling in now? Be honest in your examination. What conclusion did you come to from your efforts? If you have not come to a definite conclusion yet, reread Ecclesiastes. Know that if you continue to pursue a worldly life-style, you cannot help but reach the same place that Solomon did. Take his words as an encouragement to pursue a godly life-style.

3. Read through the verses in Proverbs on pages 26-29. As you read, make a list of the benefits that God's wisdom makes available to every believer. Which ones are you presently experiencing? Are there some you aren't experiencing to the degree you would like? Remember that although you receive God's wisdom when you become a Christian, you are still responsible to appropriate it in your life on a daily basis. To help you do so, begin a daily reading program in Proverbs. Read one chapter a day. There are thirty-one chapters in Proverbs, so you can read through the entire book in one month. When you've completed one month, read through the book again. Let God's wisdom penetrate every aspect of your life.

2
Earthly and Heavenly Wisdom—Part 2

Outline

Review
I. The Manifestation of Wisdom (v. 13)

A Bible Study on Wisdom

I. The Perspective of Human Wisdom
II. The Perspective of Godly Wisdom
  A. The Source of Wisdom
  B. The Pursuit of Wisdom

Lesson
  C. The Beginning of Wisdom
    1. The concept of fearing God
      a) Expressed
        (1) Proverbs 1:7
        (2) Proverbs 1:29
        (3) Proverbs 9:10
        (4) Proverbs 15:33
      b) Explained
      c) Exemplified
        (1) Acts 10:22
        (2) Acts 17:17
    2. The consequences of fearing God
      a) Wisdom
      b) A long and fulfilling life
        (1) Proverbs 10:27
        (2) Proverbs 14:27

33

3. The characteristics of fearing God
   a) Obedience
      (1) Psalm 111:10
      (2) John 14:15
      (3) 1 John 2:3
   b) Turning away from evil
   c) Hating evil
4. The comprehensiveness of fearing God

Conclusion

Review

James speaks of two kinds of wisdom: earthly, sensual, and demonic wisdom, which characterizes those who don't know God, and pure, peaceable, gentle, compliant, merciful, good, impartial, and sincere wisdom, which characterizes those who do know Him. The determination of which kind of wisdom a person has is a test of living faith.

I. THE MANIFESTATION OF WISDOM (see pp. 12-16)

A Bible Study on Wisdom

I. THE PERSPECTIVE OF HUMAN WISDOM (see pp. 17-22)

II. THE PERSPECTIVE OF GODLY WISDOM

A. The Source of Wisdom (see pp. 23-24)

B. The Pursuit of Wisdom (see pp. 24-29)

Lesson

C. The Beginning of Wisdom

Man searches for wisdom apart from God, but he can't find it. Only God, its author, knows all. Consequently the one

34

who knows God has access to wisdom. Job 28:28 says, "The fear of the Lord, that is wisdom." The fear of the Lord is the most basic idea related to wisdom and is the key to understanding it.

1. The concept of fearing God

The book of Proverbs teaches us that the fear of the Lord is inextricably linked to wisdom.

a) Expressed

   (1) Proverbs 1:7—"The fear of the Lord is the beginning of knowledge; fools despise wisdom and instruction." *Knowledge, wisdom, understanding,* and *instruction* are often used as synonyms in Proverbs.

   (2) Proverbs 1:29—Many people have sought wisdom but have not found it: "They hated knowledge, and did not choose the fear of the Lord." Again, the fear of the Lord is related to the wisdom and knowledge of God.

   (3) Proverbs 9:10—"The fear of the Lord is the beginning of wisdom, and the knowledge of the Holy One is understanding." Since wisdom and understanding are parallel, so are the fear of the Lord and knowledge of the Holy One. To know God and to fear God are one and the same.

   (4) Proverbs 15:33—"The fear of the Lord is the instruction for wisdom." Wisdom is inseparably linked to fearing God.

b) Explained

What does it mean to fear God? It's a reverential trust, or simply another way of describing saving faith. We begin to be wise when we revere God and trust in Him. When an Old Testament saint wanted to evangelize, he might have said, "Fear God!"

c) Exemplified

The New Testament reiterates this concept of fearing God:

(1) Acts 10:22—Cornelius the centurion was identified as "a righteous and God-fearing man." That means he was a Gentile who had converted to Judaism.

(2) Acts 17:17—Paul "was reasoning in the synagogue with the Jews and the God-fearing Gentiles." Gentile believers were considered to be "God-fearing" because they had reverential trust in the living and true God.

2. The consequences of fearing God

a) Wisdom

When you read in the Bible of people fearing God or that fearing God is linked to wisdom, that means a person cannot even begin to be wise until he is first converted. Fearing God is the initiation of a life of faith. As long as a person has only human wisdom— or to put it in James's words, that which is "earthly, natural, demonic" (3:15)—he cannot know God or true wisdom. On the other hand, when a person puts his trust in God, he takes a step toward obeying God's revealed wisdom. That's what Christian living is all about.

b) A long and fulfilling life

(1) Proverbs 10:27—"The fear of the Lord prolongs life, but the years of the wicked will be shortened." Fearing God allows a full and meaningful life that is not cut short because of evil.

(2) Proverbs 14:27—"The fear of the Lord is a fountain of life, that one may avoid the snares of death." The fear of the Lord is the same as salva-

36

tion—it becomes our life and extends it, causing us to avoid death.

The fear of the Lord is our entrance to wisdom. It prolongs our life, fulfills our life, enriches our life, and *is* our life. It opens the continual flow of God's wisdom to us. The significance of everything is tied to the wisdom of God, which alone gives us proper values, guidance, instruction, and perspective in life. Divine wisdom comes only to those who fear God by placing their reverential trust in Him.

Wisdom begins, then, with a relationship to God. I believe James assumed that. I believe his contrast between the wisdom of the world and the wisdom of God is a contrast between the unsaved and the saved (although Christians can operate using only human wisdom at times).

3. The characteristics of fearing God

a) Obedience

The wisdom of God resulting from the fear of the Lord leads to obedience. When we fear the Lord we submit to His wisdom. We aren't always as obedient as we ought to be, but the pattern of our lives turns from disobedience to a submissive heart of obedience.

(1) Psalm 111:10—"The fear of the Lord is the beginning of wisdom; a good understanding have all those who do His commandments." Having come to God in reverential trust, a believer commits himself to keeping His commandments.

(2) John 14:15—Jesus said the same thing: "If you love Me, you will keep My commandments."

(3) 1 John 2:3—"By this we know that we have come to know Him, if we keep His commandments." A person's claim to be a Christian is meaningless if he's not obedient. Saving faith is obedient faith.

True wisdom comes only from God and is given only to those who fear Him by placing their lives in His hands.

b) Turning away from evil

Job 28:28 further defines the nature of fearing God: "Behold, the fear of the Lord, that is wisdom; and to depart from evil is understanding." Equal to wisdom is understanding, and equal to fearing the Lord is departing from evil. From a positive perspective, fearing the Lord involves obeying His commandments. But from a negative one it involves turning away from evil.

c) Hating evil

Proverbs 8:13—"The fear of the Lord is to hate evil; pride and arrogance and the evil way, and the perverted mouth, I hate." This takes fearing the Lord a step further.

Obeying the Lord's commandments and shunning evil are dynamics that work in the soul of one who truly fears God. They are the elements of salvation.

4. The comprehensiveness of fearing God

I believe the essence of saving faith in the Old Testament is the fear of the Lord and its resulting wisdom. It differs little from the New Testament, where we are told to repent by turning from sin (Acts 2:38), confessing Jesus as Lord (Rom. 10:9), obeying His Word (John 14:15), and hating sin (Rom. 7:15, 19). The Old Testament provides the foundation for understanding that those who fear the Lord will obey Him and hate sin.

a) Deuteronomy 4:10—"Remember the day you stood before the Lord your God at Horeb, when the Lord said to me, 'Assemble the people to Me, that I may let them hear My words so they may learn to fear Me all the days they live on the earth, and that they may teach their children.' " God wanted His people to learn to fear Him and to teach their children to do the same. He didn't say, "I want you to be in a constant state of panic that I might blast you out of existence." He expressed His desire for a relationship with them based on reverential trust.

b) Deuteronomy 5:26-27—The Israelites asked Moses to serve as their mediator with their holy and powerful God, saying, "For who is there of all flesh, who has heard the voice of the living God speaking from the midst of the fire, as we have, and lived? Go near and hear all that the Lord our God says; then speak to us all that the Lord our God will speak to you, and we will hear and do it." At that point the people had a healthy fear of God. Certainly they knew He was a God who hated sin.

c) Deuteronomy 6:1-2, 13-15, 24—Moses addressed the Israelites, saying, "Now this is the commandment, the statutes and the judgments which the Lord your God has commanded me to teach you, that you might do them in the land where you are going over to possess it, so that you and your son and your grandson might fear the Lord your God, to keep all His statutes and His commandments, which I command you, all the days of your life, and that your days may be prolonged. . . . You shall fear only the Lord your God; and you shall worship Him, and swear by his name. You shall not follow other gods, any of the gods of the peoples who surround you, for the Lord your God in the midst of you is a jealous God. . . . So the Lord commanded us to observe all these statutes, to fear the Lord our God for our good always and for our survival." Blessing and long life are products of fearing the Lord.

d) Deuteronomy 8:6—"Therefore, you shall keep the commandments of the Lord your God, to walk in His ways and to fear Him." Rather than using the words "fear Him," we could substitute "trust Him," "believe in Him," or "commit your life to Him."

e) Deuteronomy 10:12-13—"Israel, what does the Lord your God require from you, but to fear the Lord your God, to walk in all His ways and love Him, and to serve the Lord your God with all your heart and with all your soul, and to keep the Lord's commandments and His statutes which I am commanding you today for your good." Fearing the Lord results in a life of obedience.

f) Deuteronomy 13:4—"You shall follow the Lord your God and fear Him; and you shall keep His commandments, listen to His voice, serve Him, and cling to Him."

g) Deuteronomy 14:23—"You shall eat in the presence of the Lord your God, at the place where He chooses to establish His name, the tithe of your grain, your new wine, your oil, and the first-born of your herd and your flock, in order that you may learn to fear the Lord your God always." Fearing God is not just a one-time event; it's a way of life. It's an ongoing pursuit.

h) Deuteronomy 17:19—Moses commanded that each king of Israel should read the law "all the days of his life, that he may learn to fear the Lord his God, by carefully observing all the words of this law and these statutes."

i) Deuteronomy 28:58-59—"If you are not careful to observe all the words of this law which are written in this book, to fear this honored and awesome name, the Lord your God, then the Lord will bring extraordinary plagues on you and your descendants."

j) Deuteronomy 31:12—"Assemble the people, the men and the women and children and the alien who is in your town, in order that they may hear and learn and fear the Lord your God, and be careful to observe all the words of this law."

The fear of the Lord is not some feeling you try to generate within yourself; it's the result of believing in the true God and living a life of love and obedience to Him. Deuteronomy summarizes fearing the Lord as going hand in hand with keeping His Word, obeying His commands, serving Him, loving Him, and clinging to Him. Those are different ways of saying the same thing.

Conclusion

True wisdom comes only to those who put their reverential trust in the living God, who has revealed Himself in His Son—the Lord Jesus Christ. Apart from Christ, there is no way anyone can possess the true wisdom of God. Once we have His wisdom, we also have a Teacher from God who will guide and teach us—the Holy Spirit (John 16:13). First John 2:27 says He will teach us all that is necessary, so we don't need to depend on human wisdom. We're taught of God through the Holy Spirit and through Spirit-filled human teachers who instruct us in the Word of God.

Discerning the Solutions to the World's Problems

It's amazing how easy it is for any believer to analyze the world. People who have no biblical background don't find it easy to resolve controversial issues like capital punishment, abortion, or homosexuality. But the Bible has clear answers for those seemingly complex issues: if you take a life, you should die (Gen. 9:6), the life within the womb is a person made by God (Ps. 139:13), and homosexuality is not an alternate life-style but a damning sexual sin like adultery or fornication (1 Cor. 6:9-10; Rom. 1:26-27).

Although we as Bible-believing Christians may not be considered noble or mighty by the world's standards (1 Cor. 1:26) and may be seen as the refuse of the world (1 Cor. 4:13), we've got the answers to the important questions. We have been ushered into the wisdom of God through fear of the Lord by His sovereign, gracious work.

Lawrence Toombs, in his article "O. T. Theology and the Wisdom Literature," in *The Journal of Bible and Religion*, said, "Wisdom is to be found with God and nowhere else. And unless the quest for wisdom brings a man to his knees in awe and reverence, knowing his own helplessness to make himself wise, wisdom remains for him a closed book" (23:3 [July 1955], p. 195). It's wonderful to have the book of God's wisdom opened to us.

Christians have the Spirit of wisdom and the wisdom of the Word. Therefore we can be truly wise. In Luke 11:49 God's Word is called the "wisdom of God," and in Isaiah 11:2 the Holy Spirit is called the "Spirit of wisdom." The apostle Paul said, "You are in Christ Jesus, who became to us wisdom from God" (1 Cor. 1:30). Once we fear God, His wisdom continually flows to us. Paul said to the Colossians that in Christ dwells "all the treasures of wisdom and knowledge" (2:3). Because Christ dwells in us, we can possess the very wisdom of God.

The Bible puts no premium on human wisdom. Knowledge is of no benefit until it affects behavior and conduct. True wisdom will result in obedience. Knowledge, at its deepest level, leads a person to live out a personal relationship with God. Wisdom is simply manifesting the truth of God in every dimension of life. When a believer combines the Word and Spirit of wisdom—though he may not be wise in the eyes of the world—he is wise beyond the world's wisdom. For he understands what the natural man could never understand, because the "natural man [unbeliever] does not accept the things of the Spirit of God; for they are foolishness to him, and he cannot understand them" (1 Cor. 2:14). What a marvelous privilege a believer has! At the same time, how foolish for a believer who possesses the wisdom of God to pervert himself and live according to the wisdom of the world!

Focusing on the Facts

1. Who has access to God's wisdom (see pp. 34-35)?
2. In the book of Proverbs, what concept is inextricably linked to acquiring wisdom (see p. 35)?
3. List some synonyms used for *wisdom* in Proverbs (see p. 35).
4. What does it mean to fear God (see p. 35)?
5. What are two consequences of fearing God (see pp. 36-37)?
6. What two kinds of people does James probably have in mind when he contrasts the world's wisdom with God's wisdom (see p. 37)?
7. What becomes the pattern of a life for the one who fears the Lord (see p. 37)?
8. When does a person's claim to be a Christian appear meaningless? Why (see p. 37)?
9. How will one who fears God respond toward evil? Support your answer with Scripture (see p. 38).
10. According to Deuteronomy 4:10, why did God want to speak to the Israelites (see pp. 38-39)?
11. Is fearing the Lord a one-time event? Explain (see p. 40).

12. Summarize the comprehensiveness of fearing the Lord as expressed in Deuteronomy (see p. 40).
13. Why does a Christian not need to depend on human wisdom (1 John 2:27; see p. 41)?

Pondering the Principles

1. Do you regularly exhibit the characteristics of one who fears God? Is your life characterized by obedience to God and a hatred of evil, which results in your turning away from it? In what areas of your life are you being disobedient to God? What kinds of evil are you still harboring in your life? Ask God to reveal that evil to you. Only as you see the reality of sin in your life and see how God views that sin will you develop a healthy fear of God. Remember this: Jesus Christ paid the price for your sin and ushered you into a relationship with God. Honor His work by learning to see evil from God's perspective.

2. Praise the Lord for the privilege of knowing Him and His will through His Word and His Spirit. Pray that you might manifest the wisdom of the living God so that the world sees you living a life that is pure, peaceable, reasonable, gentle, merciful, fruitful, unwavering, and without hypocrisy (James 3:17). Meditate on Matthew 5:16, James 3:13, and 1 Peter 3:14-16. Seek to demonstrate wise behavior so the world may know that the controlling force in your life is from above, and that others may seek Him to have their own lives transformed.

3
Earthly and Heavenly Wisdom—Part 3

Outline

Introduction
A. Growing in Wisdom
B. Receiving Wisdom
   1. Matthew 7:24-27
   2. Matthew 24:42-51
   3. 1 Corinthians 1:23-24, 30
   4. Colossians 2:3, 10
   5. 2 Timothy 3:15

Review
I. The Manifestation of Wisdom (v. 13)

Lesson
II. The Contrast of Wisdom (vv. 14-18)
   A. False Wisdom (vv. 14-16)
      1. The motivation (v. 14)
         a) The source of the motivation
            (1) Bitter jealousy
            (2) Selfish ambition
         b) The solution to the motivation
      2. The characteristics (v. 15)
         a) Their distinction (v. 15a)
         b) Their description (v. 15b)
            (1) "Earthly"
            (2) "Sensual"
            (3) "Demoniacal"
      3. The results (v. 16)
         a) "Confusion"
         b) "Every evil work"

B. True Wisdom (vv. 17-18)
   1. The motivation (v. 17*a*)
   2. The characteristics (v. 17*b*)
   3. The results (v. 18)

Conclusion

Introduction

The epistle of James gives a series of tests for verifying the genuineness of one's faith. James 3:13-18 contrasts earthly and heavenly wisdom, which is one of those tests. James is telling his readers that those who are truly saved—those who genuinely know God and possess a living faith—have a certain kind of wisdom. Their spiritual conversion is manifested by their wisdom. All of us who know God through Christ have received the wisdom of God. And that wisdom is manifest in the life of a true believer.

A. Growing in Wisdom

As Christians we will manifest the wisdom of God in ever-increasing amounts as we grow spiritually. A true Christian will love the Lord Jesus Christ—and should love Him even more as time goes on. The same thing goes for his service and obedience to God. Although believers have received the wisdom of God, that does not mean we are applying all the wisdom we should. None of us manifest the wisdom of God to our greatest capacity. While James 3:13-18 talks about wisdom as the mark of a believer, it also encourages and exhorts us to increase our wisdom.

B. Receiving Wisdom

The New Testament connects wisdom to believing God's Word.

1. Matthew 7:24-27—"Whosoever heareth these sayings of mine, and doeth them, I will liken him unto a wise man, who built his house upon a rock. And the rain descended, and the floods came, and the winds blew and beat upon that house, and it fell not; for it was founded upon a rock. And every one that heareth these sayings of mine,

and doeth them not, shall be likened unto a foolish man, who built his house on the sand. And the rain descended, and the floods came, and the winds blew and beat upon that house, and it fell; and great was the fall of it." The unregenerate man of verses 26-27 appears religious but has no foundation and is a fool. However, the truly converted man of verses 24-25 obeys the Word of God and is considered wise. In the words of our Lord, wisdom is equated with true salvation.

2. Matthew 24:42-51—"Watch, therefore; for ye know not what hour your Lord doth come. But know this, that if the householder had known in what watch the thief would come, he would have watched, and would not have allowed his house to be broken into. Therefore be ye also ready; for in such an hour as ye think not the Son of man cometh. Who, then, is a faithful and wise servant, whom his lord hath made ruler over his household, to give them food in due season? Blessed is that servant, whom his lord, when he cometh, shall find so doing. Verily I say to you that he shall make him ruler over all his goods. But and if that evil servant shall say in his heart, My lord delayeth his coming; and shall begin to smite his fellow servants, and to eat and drink with drunkards, the lord of that servant shall come in a day when he looketh not for him, and in an hour that he is not aware of, and shall cut him asunder, and appoint him his portion with the hypocrites; there shall be weeping and gnashing of teeth." The unregenerate man was a fool, and the man who was ready for the Lord's coming was wise.

3. 1 Corinthians 1:23-24, 30—"We preach Christ crucified, unto the Jews a stumbling block, and unto the Gentiles foolishness; but unto them who are called [to salvation], both Jews and Greeks, Christ the power of God, and the wisdom of God" (vv. 23-24). When you receive Christ, He becomes to you the wisdom of God. Verse 30 says, "But of him are ye in Christ Jesus, who of God is made unto us wisdom."

4. Colossians 2:3, 10—"In [Christ] are hidden all the treasures of wisdom and knowledge. . . . And ye are complete in him."

5. 2 Timothy 3:15—Paul tells Timothy, "From a child thou hast known the holy scriptures, which are able to make thee wise unto salvation through faith which is in Christ Jesus." Faith in Christ Jesus makes you wise.

True wisdom is an identifying mark of a saved person, and that is what James is proposing. He is saying you can know a person's spiritual status by the kind of wisdom he manifests.

Review

I. THE MANIFESTATION OF WISDOM (v. 13; see pp. 12-16)

"Who is a wise man and endued with knowledge among you? Let him show out of a good life his works with meekness of wisdom."

Lesson

II. THE CONTRAST OF WISDOM (vv. 14-18)

A. False Wisdom (vv. 14-16)

James begins his discussion by analyzing worldly wisdom, which is not of God: it has no relationship to God, is not obedient to God, and has no knowledge of God's truth.

1. The motivation (v. 14)

"But if ye have bitter envying and strife in your hearts, glory not, and lie not against the truth."

a) The source of the motivation

The source of the motive is indicated by the phrase, "in your hearts." Proverbs 4:23 says, "Keep thy heart with all diligence; for out of it are the issues of life." Two things motivate a person to adhere to human wisdom: bitter jealousy and selfish ambition (better translations of "bitter envying" and "strife").

(1) Bitter jealousy

The Greek word translated "bitter" (*pikron*) means "harsh" or "bitter." It is used of bitter, undrinkable water. The Greek word translated "envying" or "jealousy" is *zelos*. These two definitions combined carry the idea of a harsh, bitter self-centeredness that produces a resentful attitude toward others.

People with bitter jealousy live in a world that focuses on themselves. They react in a jealous manner toward anyone who threatens their territory, accomplishments, or reputation. They resent anyone who threatens to crowd their slice of this world. Self-centered people have a problem with bitter jealousy. Some handle it better than others, but they all struggle with it. They consider people who differ from them as implacable enemies. And they are bitterly jealous of anyone who is successful.

(2) Selfish ambition

The Greek word translated "strife" or "selfish ambition" is *erithian*. It refers to a personal ambition that creates rivalry, antagonism, or a party spirit. That's another way of pointing to self. The person who follows human wisdom begins with a bitter jealousy that creates an attitude of competition and conflict. Then selfish ambition generates a party spirit and bitterness toward others. *Erithian* comes from *erithos* ("hireling") and *eritheuō*, which means "to spin wool." It was used of ladies who made thread. It eventually came to refer to anyone who performed work for pay. Then it referred to anything anyone did for what he might personally gain from his effort. It was used of people who entered politics for selfish motives and of those who sought the attainment of personal goals no matter what they had to do to others to reach those goals.

James is saying that ungodly wisdom is selfish, self-centered, and consumed with ego fulfillment. Its goal is personal gratification at any cost.

b) The solution to the motivation

In verse 14 James says that if a person has a self-centered motive for life, he should "glory not." He should stop arrogantly boasting. He should stop claiming to possess true wisdom. Why? Because he is lying "against the truth." In verse 13 James indicates that if a person claims to have God's wisdom, he must show it. If I see you are motivated by self-centeredness, pride, and ego-fulfillment, you ought to stop your arrogant boasting about having the wisdom of God. The fact is you're lying against what is obviously true. Stop claiming to have what you don't have.

The "truth" refers to the saving gospel. Both James 1:18 ("Of his own will begot he us with the word of truth") and James 5:19 ("If any of you do err from the truth, and one convert him") link the truth with the gospel. Anyone who claims to have the wisdom of God but lives a life motivated by selfish ambition and bitter jealousy should stop making such an arrogant boast. He is obviously lying in the face of the gospel. No pretentious claims to a possession of divine wisdom are convincing when they come out of a heart totally motivated by jealousy and selfish ambition.

James is calling for us to take an inventory of our hearts. Take a look at yourself. What motivates you? Are you motivated by the things that honor God? Are you motivated by a love for others? Are you motivated by humility and unselfishness? Or are you on a massive ego trip to fulfill your desires? There is no single characteristic of unredeemed man more obvious than his pride. And there is nothing more characteristically evident of a redeemed person than his humility.

2. The characteristics (v. 15)

   a) Their distinction (v. 15a)

   "This wisdom descendeth not from above."

   Wisdom that is bitterly jealous and self-centered is
   not from above. Such traits constitute a wisdom that
   doesn't come from God. They don't qualify to be
   called divine. Only true wisdom comes from God.
   James 1:5 says, "If any of you lack wisdom, let him
   ask of God, who giveth to all men liberally, and upbraideth not, and it shall be given him." Verse 17
   says, "Every good gift and every perfect gift is from
   above, and cometh down from the Father of lights,
   with whom is no variableness, neither shadow of
   turning." God is the source of wisdom. He gives it to
   those who ask just as He gives all good gifts. Worldly
   wisdom—"the wisdom of men" as Paul calls it in 1
   Corinthians 1 and 2—is not from God.

   b) Their description (v. 15b)

   (1) "Earthly"

      Earthly means just that. Its extent is limited to the
      sphere of time and space. Earthly wisdom cannot
      crawl out of its locked prison. Man is trapped in a
      box of time and space. God and eternal truth are
      outside that box. All of man's wisdom is marked
      by the curse of his own fallenness, which is char-
      acterized by his pride and self-centeredness.
      Everything the world initiates in the way of sup-
      posed truth is self-centered. Unregenerate man's
      finite system demands an earthly wisdom and
      nothing more. The corruption of his system per-
      vades every dimension of his life, including his
      philosophical and educational systems.

   (2) "Sensual"

      The Greek word translated "sensual" is *psuchikē*,
      which means "fleshy." It refers to man's human-

ness and frailty. Whatever belongs to the natural world is *psuchikē*. First Corinthians 2:14 says, "The natural [Gk., *psuchikos*] man receiveth not the things of the Spirit of God." The natural man is sensual. All his feelings, impulses, and appetites are locked up in a fallen and corrupted system. All of man's wisdom is spawned from his unsanctified heart and unredeemed spirit. The fields of sociology, psychology, philosophy, and education tend in general to comprehend and solve man's problems from a humanistic, fleshy, and sensual perspective.

(3) "Demoniacal"

James 3:15 is the only place in the New Testament where the Greek word translated "demon" appears in its adjectival form. Human wisdom is actually generated by demons, who have been made captive to the same evil system as man. Earthly wisdom is spawned by demons, is reflective of man's humanness, and proceeds no further than the fallenness of mankind. The wisdom of the world is generated by Satan and his agents. They disguise themselves as ministers of light when in fact they are ministers of darkness (2 Cor. 11:14-15). The combination of man's wisdom and wickedness is deadly.

The Action of the Restrainer

Demonic, natural, earthbound wisdom never touches God. It leads man to be smug and immoral—totally abandoned to his natural impulses. The only thing that restrains the world from a barbaric, animalistic existence is God's gracious salting of the earth with divine wisdom. He has put a living restrainer on the earth—His Holy Spirit. But when the Spirit's restraining work has ceased, and when the salt (the people of God) is removed in the rapture, all hell will break loose during the seven-year period known as the Tribulation. Evil will no longer be restrained. Man will then be able to pursue immorality and evil to its fullest extent. Its malignancy will spread its killing influence everywhere.

3. The results (v. 16)

"For where envying and strife are, there is confusion and every evil work."

a) "Confusion"

The Greek word translated "confusion" (*akatastasia*) refers to disorder that comes out of instability and chaos. The same word is used in James 1:8 to refer to the impact of double-mindedness. In James 3:8 it refers to the impact of an uncontrolled tongue. Double-mindedness and an uncontrolled tongue result in chaos, confusion, and disorder. Earthly wisdom will never produce harmony or love because it is proud and self-indulgent. It destroys intimacy, love, unity, and fellowship, and in its place brings discord and chaos. You can see the result of earthly wisdom all over our world today. Anger, bitterness, lawsuits, and divorces are just part of the legacy of earthly wisdom. Confusion and disorder will grow worse as men continue to move toward the coming day when Jesus Christ returns to this world.

b) "Every evil work"

The Greek word translated "every evil work" (*phaulos*) means "worthless" or "vile." Greek scholar R. C. Trench said it contemplates evil "not so much that either of active or passive malignity, but that rather of its good-for-nothingness, the impossibility of any true gain ever coming forth from it" (*Synonyms of the New Testament* [Grand Rapids: Eerdmans, 1983], p. 317).

The Greek word translated "work" (*pragma*) means "thing." False wisdom produces nothing of any pragmatic value. At its best it produces worthless things; at its worst it produces vile things.

B. True Wisdom (vv. 17-18)

1. The motivation (v. 17a)

"But the wisdom that is from above is first pure."

The Greek word translated "pure" (*hagnē*) implies something or someone that is sincere, moral, and spiritual in character. It refers to spiritual integrity and moral sincerity. It is freedom from bitter jealousy, selfish ambition, and arrogant self-promotion. The apostle John used that word to refer to Jesus Christ (1 John 3:3). He is the pattern of all purity.

A true believer will have pure desires. The deepest part of him desires to do God's will, serve God, and love God. In Romans 7:15-21 the apostle Paul testifies that when he sinned, he was doing what he didn't want to do. In Psalm 51:7 David cries out, "Purge me with hyssop, and I shall be clean; wash me, and I shall be whiter than snow." The true believer hates his sin. Rising out of his innermost being is a longing for what is clean, and pure, and holy, and honest. He shrinks from contamination. He desires clean hands and a pure heart (Ps. 24:3-4). One of the Beatitudes indicates purity is a condition of a true believer: "Blessed are the pure in heart; for they shall see God" (Matt. 5:8).

In the Greek language the root of *hagnē* carried the idea of being pure enough in heart to approach the gods. It initially referred to ceremonial cleansing but eventually referred to the moral purity that allowed one to approach his god. Hebrews 12:14 says, "Follow . . . holiness, without which no man shall see the Lord."

The motive of the believer is a pure heart. He is not motivated by a prideful heart. God says He will "take the stony heart out of their flesh, and will give them a heart of flesh" (Ezek. 11:19); that new heart will be consumed with purity rather than self. Now you still sin, because your new heart is incarcerated in your old flesh. But your heart fights against your flesh. That's why Paul said, "I delight in the law of God after the inward man; but I see another law in my members, warring against

54

the law of my mind, and bringing me into captivity to the law of sin which is in my members" (Rom. 7:22-23).

2. The characteristics (v. 17b)

In verse 17 "then" follows "pure," setting it apart from the rest of the list. That indicates to me that James is using "pure" as a motive rather than simply a characteristic of true wisdom. So he moves on from the motive to the outward behavior—the qualities of true wisdom.

a) "Peaceable"

The Greek word translated "peaceable" (eirēnikos) means "peace loving" or "peace promoting." Matthew 5:9 says, "Blessed are the peacemakers; for they shall be called the sons of God." Wisdom from God does not create confusion or disorder. It is not self-promoting. It is peace loving and peace making. It doesn't compromise with truth; it makes peace.

b) "Gentle"

The Greek word translated "gentle" is difficult to translate accurately. One writer called it sweet reasonableness. It is a lovely attribute of redeemed character and godly wisdom. A gentle person will submit to dishonor, disgrace, mistreatment, and persecution with an attitude of humility, courteousness, kindness, patience, and consideration without hatred, malice, or revenge. Matthew 5:10-11 says, "Blessed are they who are persecuted for righteousness' sake; for theirs is the kingdom of heaven. Blessed are ye, when men shall revile you, and persecute you, and shall say all manner of evil against you falsely, for my sake."

c) "Easy to be entreated"

This is a translation of the Greek word eupeithēs. It refers to someone who is willing to yield, easily persuaded, teachable, and compliant. He is not stubborn, obstinate, and disobedient. Eupeithēs was used of a person who willingly submitted to military discipline or who observed legal and moral standards in life and willingly submitted to them. That is reflective of Matthew 5:3-5: "Blessed are the poor in spirit; for theirs is the kingdom of heaven. Blessed are they that mourn; for they shall be comforted. Blessed are the meek; for they shall inherit the earth." Those who are humble, mournful, and meek are compliant, easily persuaded, teachable, and yielding to God's standards for life.

d) "Full of mercy"

Someone who is full of mercy shows a concern for people who suffer and is quick to forgive. People who are merciful, kind, and compassionate demonstrate the Beatitude of Matthew 5:7, "Blessed are the merciful; for they shall obtain mercy."

e) "Good fruits"

"Good fruits" refer to all good works in general or a wide variety of spiritual deeds. It is much like Matthew 5:6, "Blessed are they who do hunger and thirst after righteousness." The Christian demonstrates the genuineness of his salvation through his good deeds —works that are produced by faith (James 2:14-20), known as the fruit of the Spirit (Gal. 5:22-23) and the fruit of righteousness (Phil. 1:11).

f) "Without partiality"

James 3:17 is the only place in the New Testament where the Greek word translated "without partiality" is used. It refers to someone who is unwavering and undivided in his commitment. This person doesn't vacillate. He is consistent. In James 2:1-13 James talked about the evil of being partial toward the rich. One who possesses the wisdom of God is without partiality and sincere in his faithfulness to God. He lets his "light so shine before men, that they may see [his] good works, and glorify [his] Father, who is in heaven" (Matt. 5:16). He is characterized by an unwavering commitment and doesn't make unfair distinctions.

g) "Without hypocrisy"

Someone without hypocrisy is utterly sincere and genuine. He isn't a phony or a fake. This characteristic is the climax of true wisdom. A truly wise person manifests sincere behavior.

3. The results (v. 18)

"And the fruit of righteousness is sown in peace by them that make peace."

True wisdom is equated with the fruit of righteousness because wisdom results in righteous living. At first glance it seems strange that James would say the "fruit of righteousness is sown" because usually seed is sown. But harvested fruit also becomes seed for the next crop. The fruit of righteousness is sown again in peace by those who make peace. Where true wisdom exists, true righteousness follows. And that becomes seed and generates more righteousness. That's the law of sowing and reaping. Verse 18 is in the present tense and literally reads, "The fruit of righteousness is being sown in peace by them that make peace." It is a continual cycle: one righteous act harvested from the field of true wisdom becomes the seed to grow another righteous act. Those who make peace receive the benefit from it. The phrase "by them that make peace" is vague. Perhaps we can say righteousness flourishes in a climate of peace. The bottom line is that peacemakers aren't preoccupied with themselves.

Conclusion

James follows a clear line of thought. If one professes to be a Christian, he must prove it by living like a Christian. Nothing is more convincing than the kind of wisdom revealed in his or her behavior. God's wisdom should mark those who belong to Jesus Christ.

Wisdom equals life-style. True wisdom is acquired only through faith in God through Jesus Christ. Once we are saved, Scripture becomes the source of wisdom and the Holy Spirit our teacher of wisdom.

Focusing on the Facts

1. James 3:13-18 discusses wisdom as the mark of a believer. In what way does it encourage the believer (see p. 46)?
2. Explain how Matthew 7:24-27 links wisdom with salvation (see pp. 46-47).
3. What two things motivate a person to follow human wisdom? Explain each one (see pp. 48-49).
4. What does James command for those who follow human wisdom? Why (James 3:14; see p. 50)?
5. From where does true wisdom come (see p. 51)?
6. Describe how man's wisdom can be considered earthly (see p. 51).
7. Why is man's wisdom considered sensual (see pp. 51-52)?
8. How can man's wisdom be demoniacal (see p. 52)?
9. What restrains the people of the world from living a barbaric existence (see p. 52)?
10. What are the results of earthly wisdom? Explain each one (James 3:16; see p. 53).
11. What motivates a true believer? Explain (see p. 54).
12. What are the characteristics of a person who has true wisdom? Explain (James 3:17; see pp. 55-57).
13. What is the result of true wisdom (James 5:18; see p. 57)?

Pondering the Principles

1. Are you motivated by pride and self-indulgence? Be honest in your evaluation. James 3:14 should make every believer take a serious inventory of his heart. How many times do you honor God instead of exalting yourself? How many times do you serve others instead of fulfilling your own desires at the expense of others? Ask God to convict you when you put yourself before God and others. Repent of any present situations where you are doing that very thing.

2. Read Matthew 5:1-16 and James 3:17. Make a list of both the motives and characteristics of godly wisdom. Next to each list the
   verses from the Matthew passage that correspond to each one.
   Make it a goal to memorize the Matthew verses this week. As
   you do so, work on developing those characteristics in your life.
   But before you do, make sure you are being motivated by a pure
   heart.

4
Walking in Wisdom—Part 1

Outline

Introduction
A. The Characteristics of Foolishness
   1. A fool denies God
   2. A fool becomes his own god
   3. A fool mocks sin
   4. A fool is quick to air his opinions
   5. A fool propagates his foolishness to others
   6. A fool rejects divine wisdom
B. The Consequence of Foolishness
   1. Proverbs 1:20-32
   2. Proverbs 10:21
C. The Cure for Foolishness
D. The Contrast of Foolishness

Lesson
I. The Believer's Life Principles (v. 15)
A. The Possession of Wisdom
   1. 1 Corinthians 1:30
   2. Colossians 2:3
   3. Titus 2:11-12
   4. Ephesians 1:7-8
   5. 1 John 2:20, 27
B. The Progress of Wisdom
   1. Worship
   2. Prayer
   3. Instruction
   4. Study
C. The Perspective of Wisdom
D. The Practice of Wisdom

Introduction

There's no question in my mind that we live in a world of fools. In fact, everyone born into this world comes in with congenital foolishness—otherwise known as the sin nature. Proverbs 22:15 says, "Foolishness in bound in the heart of a child." Man is born in a state of foolishness.

Normally when we think of a fool, we think of someone who acts or speaks irresponsibly. But the Bible defines a fool as one who exists apart from God. Conversely, a wise man is one who lives in accord with divine principles. Since man is born separated from God, he's born a fool.

A. The Characteristics of Foolishness

Psalms and Proverbs paint an accurate picture of a fool:

1. A fool denies God

    Psalm 14:1 says, "The fool hath said in his heart, There is no God. They are corrupt, they have done abominable works, there is none that doeth good." I call this practical atheism. A fool lives as if there were no God—denying God with his actions.

2. A fool becomes his own god

    Proverbs 12:15 says, "The way of a fool is right in his own eyes." No man can live without a god. It isn't a question of *does* he worship; it's a question of *whom* does he worship. If a person doesn't worship the true God he will worship a false god—which will inevitably be a reflection of himself. He becomes the one who determines truth and error—articulating his own standards for living.

3. A fool mocks sin

    Proverbs 14:9 says, "Fools make a mock of sin." Since a fool makes his own rules, he wants to justify his own behavior to make sure he's going to be all right in the end. He eliminates sin along with its consequences.

A fool, then, begins by living as if there were no God, substituting himself as god, and determining his own style of life. Then he denies the existence of sin because he cannot tolerate guilt.

4. A fool is quick to air his opinions

Proverbs 15:2 says, "The tongue of the wise useth knowledge aright, but the mouth of fools poureth out foolishness." A bitter fountain produces bitter water, a rotten tree produces rotten fruit, and a fool produces foolishness—speaking on his own authority and generating his own opinions.

The world is full of the opinions of fools—fools who have denied God in their living, who have become their own gods, and who mock the reality and consequences of sin.

5. A fool propagates his foolishness to others

Proverbs 16:22 tells us that "the instruction of fools is folly." Not only does a fool generate his own authority and live his life based on his own opinions, but he also contaminates the rest of society with the same foolishness that damns his own soul. He leaves it as a legacy to his children, his friends, and all those who fall under the influence of his folly.

6. A fool rejects divine wisdom

Proverbs 1:7 says, "The fear of the Lord is the beginning of knowledge, but fools despise wisdom and instruction." Wisdom, as defined in the book of Proverbs, is living by divine standards, which implies accepting divine truth. But a fool rejects that. First Corinthians 2:14 says that "the natural man receiveth not the things of the Spirit of God; for they are foolishness unto him." To a fool, foolishness is wisdom and wisdom is foolishness.

B. The Consequence of Foolishness

What happens to a fool? What becomes of an individual who denies God, substitutes himself for God, mocks sin, spins out his own opinions, contaminates others with his foolishness, and totally rejects divine wisdom?

1. Proverbs 1:20-32—"Wisdom crieth outside; she uttereth her voice in the streets; she crieth in the chief place of concourse, in the openings of the gates; in the city she uttereth her words, saying, How long, ye simple ones, will ye love simplicity? And the scoffers delight in their scoffing, and fools hate knowledge? Turn you at my reproof; behold, I will pour out my spirit unto you, I will make known my words unto you. Because I have called, and ye refused; I have stretched out my hand, and no man regarded, but ye have set at nought all my counsel, and would have none of my reproof, I also will laugh at your calamity; I will mock when your fear cometh; when your fear cometh as desolation, and your destruction cometh as a whirlwind; when distress and anguish come upon you. Then shall they call upon me, but I will not answer; they shall seek me early, but they shall not find me; because they hated knowledge, and did not choose the fear of the Lord. They would have none of my counsel; they despised all my reproof. Therefore they shall eat of the fruit of their own way, and be filled with their own devices. For the turning away of the simple shall slay them, and the prosperity of fools shall destroy them." That is the end of it all. That is what it's like to die a fool.

2. Proverbs 10:21—"Fools die for lack of wisdom." The consequence of foolishness is death. People who live as fools die as fools.

C. The Cure for Foolishness

As we previously saw in Proverbs 1, wisdom is available to all. God reaches out His hand and offers to take people out of a kingdom of fools into the kingdom of the wise. Salvation is the only cure for foolishness.

In 2 Timothy 3:15 the apostle Paul reminds Timothy of his heritage: "From a child thou hast known the holy scriptures, which are able to make thee *wise unto salvation* through faith which is in Christ Jesus" (emphasis added). Wisdom is found in the knowledge of scriptural truth, which brings salvation. The only thing that can cause an individual to cease being a fool and to become wise is salvation. When we become Christians, we stop our foolishness and become God's wise children.

D. The Contrast of Foolishness

The Greeks saw wisdom primarily as head knowledge. They tended to spin off theories that had no practical implications. To them, the wise people were the intellectuals and the philosophers. The Hebrew mind, however, didn't tend to conceive of wisdom in theory; it defined wisdom only in terms of behavior. When a person becomes a Christian it's more than merely a change in theory—it's a change in how he lives. Before conversion, he doesn't know God, he denies God, he substitutes himself for God, he mocks sin, he spews out his own opinions, and he corrupts society. But when he becomes a Christian he immediately knows God, takes himself off the throne and worships only Him, confesses sin, speaks "the oracles of God" (1 Pet. 4:11), and instructs others with divine truth when he speaks. That's a big difference! Christians live in wisdom, not foolishness.

The apostle Paul is saying in Ephesians 5:15: "If you used to be a fool but you've been made wise in Christ, then walk wisely." In other words, we're to practice our position—to live in accordance with who we are. When we became Christians we came out of foolishness into wisdom. Therefore we need to act like it!

Be Different

Walking in wisdom is another element of the worthy walk that Paul has been describing since the beginning of chapter 4. He says in verse 1, "Walk worthy of the vocation to which ye are called," and then proceeds to describe this worthy walk with the following characteristics: it's a *humble* walk (4:1-3), a *united* walk (4:4-16), a *unique* walk (4:17-32), a *loving* walk (5:1-7), an *illuminated* walk (5:8-14), and a *wise* walk (5:15-17). The point that Paul is making in describing the various elements of the worthy walk is that Christians are different from the world. The world can't be humble because everyone is fighting for his rights. The world can't be united because it celebrates and exalts differences. The world can't be unique because it is trapped in its own self-destruction. The world can't love because it doesn't have the life of God—the source of real love. The world can't know light because it lies in the system of darkness. And the world can't be wise because the wisdom of God is hidden from the mind of man. As Paul says in 2 Timothy 3:7, "Ever learning, and never able to come to the knowledge of the truth."

In Ephesians 5:15-17 Paul discusses the fact that a believer is no longer a fool but is wise. The believer who walks in wisdom knows three things: he knows what the rules are for his life, he knows his time is limited, and he knows specifically what God wants him to do. In other words, he knows his life principles, his limited privileges, and his Lord's purposes. We'll look at those three characteristics of a Christian who walks wisely.

Lesson

I. THE BELIEVER'S LIFE PRINCIPLES (v. 15)

"See, then, that ye walk circumspectly, not as fools but as wise."

A. The Possession of Wisdom

The first two words in this verse take us backwards to Paul's invitation to become saved in verse 14: "Awake thou that sleepest, and arise from the dead, and Christ shall give thee light." In verse 15 Paul is saying, "If you have awaked from sleep, arisen from the dead, and are now in the light, then walk wisely." In other words, "Because you are saved, you are to walk in wisdom." Someone may say, "Wait a minute! How can a brand-new believer walk in wisdom? Doesn't he grow into that? Haven't wise Christians been saved many years?" Such questions miss the point of the passage. Paul is saying, "Since you are awake, alive, and in the light, you *can* walk wisely." Does a person receive enough wisdom when he's saved to be responsible for his behavior? Yes. I believe the moment an individual becomes saved, God deposits enough wisdom in him to make him absolutely responsible for his behavior.

66

1. 1 Corinthians 1:30—"But of him are ye in Christ Jesus, who of God is made unto us wisdom, and righteousness, and sanctification, and redemption." When we received Christ we simultaneously received wisdom, righteousness, sanctification, and redemption. We don't get redeemed first and receive those things later. At the moment of salvation we are made wise, righteous, and sanctified. I believe that the moment we're saved the wisdom of God takes up residence in us and we become accountable to His principles.

2. Colossians 2:3—"In whom [Christ] are hidden all the treasures of wisdom and knowledge." We are in Christ, and all the treasures of wisdom and knowledge are in Him. Consequently, Colossians 2:10 says, "Ye are complete in him."

   The moment we come to Christ we are complete. No one is saved without being given wisdom, righteousness, and sanctification. That's why I have problems with the current teachings of "easy believism." There's no consideration of the reality of what happens at the moment of salvation. People sometimes say, "If we can just get them to believe in Jesus, they'll be OK. We'll talk about righteousness, sanctification, and wisdom later on." However, simultaneous to redemption is righteousness, sanctification, and wisdom. We receive them all at the point of salvation.

3. Titus 2:11-12—"For the grace of God that bringeth salvation hath appeared to all men, teaching us that, denying ungodliness and worldly lusts, we should live soberly, righteously, and godly, in this present age." Saving grace alone teaches us all those things. A person can't say, "I'm saved—I just don't know what it means." If he's saved, salvation alone teaches him to deny ungodliness and worldly lusts and to live soberly, righteously, and godly in this present age. Anyone who's saved knows those things.

   If you're redeemed you possess wisdom. You don't have to wait till you've been saved five, ten, or forty years. You already possess it!

4. Ephesians 1:7-8—When God came into our lives we received "redemption through his blood" and "the forgiveness of sins, according to the riches of his grace." Right at the moment of salvation, God "abounded toward us in all wisdom." That's why the Christian is responsible for what he does, because God's basic life principles are given to him at salvation.

5. 1 John 2:20, 27—"But ye have an unction from the Holy One, and ye know all things. . . . But the anointing which ye have received of him abideth in you, and ye need not that any man teach you; but as the same anointing teacheth you of all things, and is truth, and is no lie, and even as it hath taught you, ye shall abide in him." We don't need to have human teachers imparting to us their human philosophy. The Holy Spirit teaches us who abide in Him all things.

If you're a Christian you have wisdom. You're no longer a fool; you're wise. And on that basis Paul says, "Walk as wise. Live according to the wisdom that you possess."

B. The Progress of Wisdom

You may be asking, "Shouldn't we aquire more wisdom?" Yes, we should. No matter how much of God's wisdom we have, we should always hunger for more. The Bible tells us that we have all the principles we need to walk in wisdom, yet there's much more available to us. We should "grow in grace, and in the knowledge of our Lord and Savior, Jesus Christ" (2 Pet. 3:18), and we should be more and more conformed to the image of Christ by the transforming work of the Spirit of God. Our wisdom should increase, as should our godliness, but we are given the basic principles at salvation. Even though a person may not know all the truths in the Bible, God's Spirit, who is resident in him from the moment of salvation, will convict and convince him of righteousness and sin.

What do you do if you want more wisdom?

1. Worship—Proverbs 9:10 says, "The fear of the Lord is the beginning of wisdom."

2. Prayer—James 1:5 says, "If any of you lack wisdom, let him ask of God, who giveth to all men liberally, and upbraideth not, and it shall be given him."

3. Instruction—Paul's instruction involved "warning every man, and teaching every man in all wisdom" so that he might "present every man perfect in Christ Jesus" (Col. 1:28). If you want more wisdom, one good way to receive it is to be instructed by someone who is wise.

4. Study—In 2 Timothy 2:15 Paul says, "Study to show thyself approved unto God, a workman that needeth not to be ashamed, rightly dividing the word of truth." Another way to gain more wisdom is to study.

C. The Perspective of Wisdom

In verse 15 of Ephesians 5 Paul says, "See, then, that ye walk circumspectly." The Greek word translated *walk* means "daily conduct," "daily pattern," or "daily life." The Jewish concept of wisdom referred to behavior, not theory.

The word *circumspectly* means "accurately," "carefully," or "exactly." To be circumspect is to look carefully from side to side, being alert to what is going on. We need to be extremely alert, because the world we're walking through is a literal mine field. Therefore we must walk circumspectly, carefully, exactly, and accurately. The wise Christian carefully charts his course according to life principles designed by God. He does not trip over the obstacles that Satan puts in his path or fall into the entanglement of the world's system. He is careful.

D. The Practice of Wisdom

Paul is basically saying in verse 15, "Since you are awake, arisen, and in the light, you have God's wisdom resident within you. Now live that way." Paul similarly instructed the Philippians when he said, "Only let your conduct be as it becometh the gospel of Christ" (Phil. 1:27). In other words, our walk should match our position.

We are far too wise and far too accountable to walk like fools. When a Christian sins and falls into the garbage of the world, he plays the fool needlessly. In Titus 3:3-8 Paul says, "We ourselves also were once foolish, disobedient, deceived, serving various lusts and pleasures, living in malice and envy, hateful, and hating one another. But after the kindness and love of God, our Savior, toward man appeared, not by works of righteousness which we have done, but according to his mercy he saved us, by the washing of regeneration, and renewing of the Holy Spirit, which he shed on us abundantly through Jesus Christ, our Savior, that, being justified by his grace, we should be made heirs according to the hope of eternal life. This is a faithful saying, and these things I will that thou affirm constantly, that they who have believed in God might be careful to maintain good works." Our transformation demands that we live our lives with care. We are too wise to walk as fools.

How Do God's People Play the Fool?

There's no excuse for one of God's children to lower himself to the level of a fool who doesn't know God or His truth—yet it happens. When King Saul was faced with being caught in his own sin, he cowered with guilt and cried out to David, "Behold, I have played the fool" (1 Sam. 26:21).

In 2 Samuel 24 David himself became vain and decided to count all his people to make a big impression on the world. His heart was puffed up, but God poured conviction on it like hot oil, burning him deeply. Second Samuel 24:10 says, "David's heart smote him after he had numbered the people. And David said unto the Lord, I have sinned greatly in what I have done: and now, I beseech thee, O Lord, take away the iniquity of thy servant; for I have done very foolishly!" David played the fool.

Moses looked out at the belligerent children of Israel who had failed God so many times, and said, "Do ye thus requite the Lord, O foolish people and unwise?" (Deut. 32:6). The Israelites played the fool.

Sadly, God's people continue to play the fool.

1. Disbelief—On the road to Emmaus, Jesus appeared to two disciples who were moaning and groaning because their Lord had been crucified and they didn't believe that He had risen from the dead. Jesus said to them, "O foolish ones, and slow of heart to believe all that the prophets have spoken!" (Luke 24:25). The first way to play the fool is to disbelieve God and His Word.

2. Disobedience—In Galatians 3:1 Paul says, "O foolish Galatians, who hath bewitched you, that ye should not obey the truth?" And in verse 3 he says, "Are ye so foolish? Having begun in the Spirit, are ye now made perfect by the flesh?" They started out well, but they were disobedient and got caught up in the works of the law.

3. Desire for the wrong things—First Timothy 6:9 says, "They that will be rich fall into temptation and a snare, and into many foolish and hurtful lusts." If you desire the wrong things, you play the fool.

4. Doing the wrong things—James 3:13-17 says, "Who is a wise man and endued with knowledge among you? Let him show out of a good life his works with meekness of wisdom. But if ye have bitter envying and strife in your hearts, glory not, and lie not against the truth. This wisdom descendeth not from above, but is earthly, sensual, demoniacal. For where envying and strife are, there is confusion and every evil work. But the wisdom that is from above is first pure, then peaceable, gentle, and easy to be entreated, full of mercy and good fruits, without partiality, and without hypocrisy."

A child of God can play the fool by disbelief, disobedience, desiring the wrong things, and doing the wrong things. It's sad to see so many Christians acting that way. It doesn't make sense. Why should Christians live as blind, ignorant, foolish people when they have the wisdom of God?

Paul says at the end of Romans, "I would have you wise unto that which is good, and simple [foolish] concerning evil" (16:19). If you have to be a fool at all, be a fool about evil.

What Are You Committed To?

I'm amazed at how devoted people can be to what they believe is important. There are many people outside Christianity who live in rigid conformity to a lot of meaningless rules.

1. Communists live in rigid conformity to rules predicated on a denial of divine revelation. They walk circumspectly and toe the mark.

2. Some cultists are so rigid and walk so circumspectly according to the principles dictated to them that if they're told they can't get married or can't be with their spouses, they conform. They're made to live in abstinence from physical relationships, follow strict diets, fast, and so on.

3. Some attempt to attain spirituality through such self-disciplined acts as lying on a bed of nails or walking through hot coals.

4. Some go through tremendous self-discipline through dieting, running, fasting, and so on.

5. Athletes discipline their bodies in all sorts of ways, involving great sacrifice.

People disciplined in things that are ultimately meaningless may be lax in things that count. I know people who run three miles every day but will not bother to read the Bible regularly. I know people who cannot discipline themselves to feed on the Word of God but stick rigorously to a diet. Many Christians are bound at the shrine of the body and are so conformed to the world's system that they're careless and lazy about conforming to Christ.

The wise Christian knows what pleases God, watches for Satan's traps, resists the devil, defeats temptation, and is selective about his behavior. In other words, he doesn't walk as a fool; he walks in wisdom—living by God's standards.

Focusing on the Facts

1. How does the Bible define a fool (see p. 62)?
2. How does Scripture characterize a fool? Explain each characteristic (see pp. 62-63).
3. What is the consequence of foolishness (see pp. 63-64)?
4. What is the only cure for foolishness (see pp. 64-65)?
5. How did the Hebrew mind conceive of wisdom? How does that perspective impact a Christian (see p. 65)?
6. Based on the characteristics the apostle Paul delineates in Ephesians 4:1–5:17, describe how the Christian is to be different from worldly people (see pp. 65-66).
7. How is a brand-new Christian able to walk in wisdom (see p. 66)?
8. According to 1 Corinthians 1:30, what does a person receive when he becomes a Christian (see p. 67)?
9. According to Colossians 2:10, what happens the moment a person comes to Christ (see p. 67)?
10. According to Titus 2:11-12, what does a believer's salvation teach him (see p. 67)?
11. Why is a Christian responsible for all that he does (Eph. 1:7-8; see p. 68)?
12. How can a believer acquire more wisdom (see pp. 68-69)?
13. Explain what Paul meant when he said the believer should "walk circumspectly" (Eph. 5:15; see p. 69).
14. What does the transformation of a believer's life demand from him (see p. 70)?
15. Cite some examples of how God's people in the past played the fool (see p. 70).
16. In what ways can Christians play the fool? Explain each way (see p. 71).

Pondering the Principles

1. Review the sections on the characteristics of foolishness and playing the fool (see pp. 62-63, 70-71). As we have seen, unbelievers aren't the only ones who do foolish things. Sometimes believers manifest characteristics of their previous life-styles. Which characteristics do you manifest? Are you guilty of deny-

ing God with your actions? Have you set up your own standards of living? Do you justify your behavior? Do you give your opinion on different issues without consulting what the Bible says about those issues? Do you influence others with unscriptural opinions? Finally, do you reject what God has to say about your life-style? Be thorough in your self-examination. If you have been guilty of any of those characteristics, confess them to God. Seek His wisdom on how you might turn from your sin. Study God's Word, replacing your standards for life with God's. Begin today!

2. Second Peter 3:18 commands believers to "grow in grace, and in the knowledge of our Lord and Savior, Jesus Christ." One of the ways we can grow is by acquiring more wisdom. Review the section on ways to acquire wisdom (see pp. 68-69). How might you practically apply those methods in your life? Make it your goal to have a worshipful heart throughout each day. Make it your continual prayer to ask God for more of His wisdom. At every opportunity take classes or sit under a Bible teacher who can instruct you in God's Word. Finally, let the Holy Spirit teach you by setting up your own regular Bible study time.

5
Walking in Wisdom—Part 2

Outline

Introduction
A. The Boundary of Time
   1. 1 Peter 1:17
   2. Job 14:14b
   3. Acts 20:24b
   4. Hebrews 12:1b
   5. 2 Timothy 4:7
B. The Brevity of Life
   1. Psalm 89:46-47a
   2. 1 Corinthians 7:29a
   3. Psalm 39:4-5a
   4. James 4:13-14

Review
I. The Believer's Life Principles (v. 15)
A. The Possession of Wisdom
B. The Progress of Wisdom
C. The Perspective of Wisdom
D. The Practice of Wisdom

Lesson
II. The Believer's Limited Privileges (v. 16)
A. Securing Opportunity
B. Suppressing Opportunity
   1. Generally
   2. Specifically
      a) The evil in Ephesus
      b) The extinction of the church

C. Seeking Opportunity
D. Squandering Opportunity
III. The Lord's Purposes (v. 17)

Introduction

Many people never finish what they begin. There are unfinished symphonies, unfinished paintings, and unfinished sculptures (sometimes because the composer or artist died). There are relationships that never become all they could be, ministries that never come to fruition, dreams that always remain dreams, and hopes that always remain hopes. For a lot of people life can be an unfinished symphony or a dream without reality—but it doesn't have to be that way. I believe the answer can be found in the phrase "redeeming the time," which is taken from the middle of our present text, Ephesians 5:15-17.

If we are ever to turn our dreams into realities and our hopes into facts—to finish our symphonies, paint our paintings, and sculpt our sculptures—it's going to occur only when we have redeemed the time. I believe that in eternity past, God prescribed the specific time that we are to live. And only as we maximize that time can we maintain its potential for fulfillment.

A. The Boundary of Time

Notice the phrase "redeeming *the* time" in verse 16. It's interesting how many times the Holy Spirit uses a definite article when He talks about this concept of time. It is "*the* time," not *a* time, *some* time, or *any* time. It's as if God has prescribed times in accurate and sovereignly determined doses, giving us each a definite time.

1. 1 Peter 1:17—"If ye call on the Father, who without respect of persons judgeth according to every man's work, pass *the time* of your sojourning here in fear" (emphasis added). In other words, Peter is saying that we have a definite set period of time, bounded by God's sovereign choice.

2. Job 14:14—"All the days of *my appointed time* will I wait, till my change come" (emphasis added). Job had a sense of an appointed time for living.

3. Acts 20:24—Paul said, "Neither count I my life dear unto myself, so that I might finish *my course* [lit., "the course of me"]" (emphasis added). In other words, God has given us a time boundary, and within that time He has defined a course. Paul in effect said, "I want to finish the specific course and the specific ministry in the specific time given to me."

4. Hebrews 12:1—"Let us lay aside every weight, and the sin which doth so easily beset us, and let us run with patience *the race* that is set before us [lit., "the set before us race"]" (emphasis added). A race implies there is a specific beginning and ending—a boundary.

5. 2 Timothy 4:7—The apostle Paul constantly desired to fulfill God's will, thus he could say at the end of his life, "I have fought a good fight, I have finished *my course* [lit., "the course"], I have kept the faith." Again, the course is a bounded period of time.

I believe God has sovereignly given each of us a specific period of time. He knows the beginning and the end because He predetermined both.

B. The Brevity of Life

1. Psalm 89:46-47—David had a tremendous sense of time and the urgency that time places on us. He cried out to God with these words: "How long, Lord? Wilt thou hide thyself forever? Shall thy wrath burn like fire? Remember how *short* my time is!" (emphasis added). In the midst of his distress, anxiety, and pain, he felt diverted from what he ought to be doing, so he said, "God, how long do I have to be off-center? I only have so much time."

2. 1 Corinthians 7:29—The apostle Paul said, "But this I say, brethren, The time is *short*" (emphasis added).

3. Psalm 39:4-5—David said, "Lord, make me to know mine end, and the measure of my days, what it is, that I may know how frail I am. Behold, thou hast made my days as an handbreadth, and mine age is as nothing before thee."

4. James 4:13-14—"Come now, ye that say, Today or tomorrow we will go into such a city, and continue there a year, and buy and sell, and get gain; whereas ye know not what shall be on the next day. For what is your life? It is even a vapor that appeareth for a *little* time, and then vanisheth away" (emphasis added).

The whole aspect of life is built around time in Ephesians 5:15-17. The topic of wisdom in verse 15 prompts Paul to write about time in verse 16. Why? Because the greatest squandering of wisdom occurs in the improper use or lack of use of our time.

Review

In our last lesson we began to look at another aspect of the worthy walk—wisdom. What does it mean to walk in wisdom? I believe the key is in redeeming the time. For the sake of Christ, and for the sake of who we are in Him, we are to use our time wisely.

In verses 15-17 Paul tells us that a Christian who walks in wisdom knows three realities: his life principles, his limited privileges, and his Lord's purposes.

I. THE BELIEVER'S LIFE PRINCIPLES (v. 15)

"See, then, that ye walk circumspectly, not as fools but as wise."

Walking in wisdom means that we conform to certain standards of living. Remember that the concept of wisdom used here in this passage is the Jewish concept, not the Greek. To the Greeks wisdom was basically an intellectual exercise. But to a Hebrew wisdom was a living principle—and that's what Paul is talking about. He's not talking about thinking, he's talking about living. Walking in wisdom is simply living according to divine principles.

A. The Possession of Wisdom (see pp. 66-68)

We saw in our last lesson that when we become Christians we instantaneously receive God's wisdom and become accountable to it. At salvation Christ "is made unto us wisdom" (1 Cor. 1:30); and Colossians 2:3 tells us that in Christ "are hidden all the treasures of wisdom and knowledge." Consequently, Colossians 2:10 says, "Ye are complete in him." From the moment of salvation wisdom is a part of our life. In Ephesians 5:15, then, Paul is saying, "Since you have become wise, walk in wisdom."

B. The Progress of Wisdom (see pp. 68-69)

Even though we are given enough wisdom at salvation to be accountable to God's principles, we are to increase in wisdom through worship (Prov. 9:10), prayer (James 1:5), instruction (Col. 1:28), and study (2 Tim. 2:15).

C. The Perspective of Wisdom (see p. 69)

The phrase translated "walk circumspectly" in verse 15 literally means "to walk accurately, carefully, or with exactness." In other words, when we become Christians we don't merely indiscriminately stroll through life doing whatever we want; there is an exactness to how we are to walk. We entered by the narrow gate, and we must walk along the narrow path of God's life principles.

D. The Practice of Wisdom (see pp. 69-72)

If the Old Testament had been written after the New Testament, we'd have reason to think that Proverbs 2 was a commentary on Ephesians 5:15. All the way through the chapter, Proverbs 2 talks about walking in wisdom, knowledge, and understanding by following the precepts of God; and not going into the way of the wicked or straying into the path of evil men. We are to walk in wisdom—to live by divine principles.

A Fool's Confusion

The world we live in is a fool's paradise. That makes it difficult to walk in wisdom. The world is constantly trying to pull us off the narrow path into its foolishness, believing that it is wise. In fact, worldly people believe that Christians are fools, and that they are wise (1 Cor. 1:18)—but it's the reverse. All of us were fools before we came to Christ, but when we came to Him we became wise. We're not the brightest, noblest, or mightiest people in the world —but we are the wisest. God has given us His wisdom in Christ.

The world is foolish. All people innately have the knowledge of God (Rom. 1:19-20), but "they glorified him not as God, neither were thankful, but became vain in their imaginations, and their foolish heart was darkened. Professing themselves to be wise, they became fools" (vv. 21-22). In what way were they fools? The greatest fool in the world is the person who says there is no God—either verbally or by the way he lives his life. Someone who doesn't believe he has to live by God's standards is the biggest fool of all.

Basically Paul is saying in Ephesians 5:15, "Since you are the wise, walk in wisdom." It doesn't make sense to have the wisdom of God dwelling in us and continue to walk as fools.

Lesson

II. THE BELIEVER'S LIMITED PRIVILEGES (v. 16)

"Redeeming the time, because the days are evil."

Our privileges are limited by time. All we have is the present. The opportunities we lose will never return to us. The Greek word translated "time" refers to opportunity. Paul doesn't use the Greek word *chronos*, which refers to time in terms of a clock or calendar; he uses the word *kairos*, which means "eras," "epochs," or "periods"—in a word, "opportunity." We are to redeem the opportunities that can be grasped for God, for His glory.

What Does Opportunity Look Like?

In one of the cities of ancient Greece stood a statue carved by Lysippos, a famous Greek sculptor from the fourth century B.C. The statue had wings on its feet, a great lock of hair on its forehead, and was bald on the back of its head. This is how it was described:

> Who . . . was thy sculptor?
> Lysippos. . . .
> And who art thou?
> Occasion [or opportunity], the all-subduer. . . .
> Why hast thou wings . . . on thy feet?
> I fleet on the wings of the wind. . . .
> And thy hair, why grows it in front?
> For him that meets me, to seize . . . .
> And why is the back of thy head bald?
> Because none may clutch me from behind, howsoe'er he desire it, when once my winged feet have darted past him. (Gisela Richter, *The Sculpture and Sculptors of the Greeks* [New Haven: Yale, 1950], pp. 283-84)

The believer who walks in wisdom always knows how to make the most of every opportunity.

A. Securing Opportunity

Paul talks about walking wisely in verse 15 and then immediately talks about taking advantage of one's opportunities in verse 16. Why does he connect those two thoughts? Because a person plays the fool with time and opportunity more than he plays the fool with any other thing. The greatest category of foolishness is the misuse of time and opportunity—and I believe he is speaking to Christians here.

The psalmist in Psalm 90:12 says, "Teach us to number our days, that we may apply our hearts unto wisdom." Wisdom numbers the days, accounts the limited time, and buys the opportunity. Wisdom shuns opportunities for evil but grasps opportunities for good.

B. Suppressing Opportunity

At the end of verse 16 Paul tells us why it's important to walk wise and redeem the time: "because the days are evil." If we are going to make anything out of an evil day, we're going to have to take advantage of our opportunities.

1. Generally

In general, the days we live in are full of evil, and the opportunities for righteousness are few. When opportunities for goodness do come, we should seize them. When God gives us an opportunity to glorify Him (which in turn will bring a blessing on us) we must take the opportunity for His name's sake. We must seize it in the midst of the evil day.

Can you imagine how it breaks God's heart to create a perfect world, filled with every good thing, and then see it become as corrupt, debauched, and vile as it is today? Can you imagine how it must be for God to watch Christians who, in the midst of this evil world, are given opportunity after opportunity to do good, yet bypass them without notice? The days are evil, and God gives us these opportunities to make things happen that matter—to fill up at least one moment of every day with something good, something righteous, something for Him.

There's a general sense in which I see this phrase in verse 16. I see God's heart broken over the evil of a world that He made for His own glory, and I say to myself, *If God gives me one small opportunity in the midst of an evil day to do something good, something to honor Him, or something to glorify Him, I'm going to grab that opportunity.* The days are evil, and it seems as though goodness is so scarce that we need to take every opportunity we can.

2. Specifically

The evil days referred to in verse 16 may be a more direct statement to the Christians in Ephesus who were reading this. Their society was particularly corrupt.

a) The evil in Ephesus

It was a day of:

(1) False doctrine and deceivers (4:14)

(2) Lasciviousness (perverted sexual desire), uncleanliness, and greed (4:19)

(3) Lying (4:25)

(4) Anger and wrath (4:26)

(5) Stealing (4:28)

(6) Corrupt communication (4:29)

(7) Bitterness, wrath, anger, clamor, and evil speaking (4:31)

(8) Fornication, uncleanness, and covetousness (5:3)

(9) Filthiness, foolish talking, and jesting (5:4)

It was certainly a day of evil, so Paul may have been alluding to the very hour in which the Ephesians were living. Persecution and distress were on the horizon. In fact, soon after this time, Christians were burned at the stake and thrown to the lions. Their days were evil, and their time was short.

b) The extinction of the church

A little more than thirty years after this letter was written, the apostle John wrote to the Ephesian church, saying, "Thou hast left thy first love . . . repent, and do the first works, or else I [Christ] will come unto thee quickly, and will remove thy lampstand out of its place, except thou repent" (Rev. 2:4-5). But the Ephesians did not repent, and the lampstand was removed. Their time was shorter than they believed, because the evil was so great. The church fell under its spell and eventually went out of existence. The time was short, the days were evil, and they fell prey to the time in which they lived.

Do You Have a Proper Sense of Urgency?

I believe we need to have a sense of urgency in the evil days in which we live. I don't know what's going to happen to Christianity in America, but I've asked God that if it takes persecution to bring us to the place where we get a grip on what we ought to be, then let it happen. In many cases throughout history, the church has thrived better under persecution than it has under affluence. As the church Father Tertullian once said, "The blood of martyrs is the seed of the church" (*Apology* 50.13).

I'm not specifically asking that the church be persecuted; I'm saying that sometimes we don't sense the urgency of our evil day because we are sucked into the system, and the lines aren't clearly drawn. It's an evil day in which we live, and the time is short. We need to realize that "evil men and seducers shall become worse and worse" (2 Tim. 3:13). It's not going to become better. The world is blacker and more expressive of its vices than ever before. We must have a sense of urgency and redeem the time.

C. Seeking Opportunity

The word translated *redeem* is in the middle voice in the Greek text and means "buy up for yourself." You are not to hoard your time for your own use; rather you are to "buy up for yourself" time that will give God glory. When you do that you will profit, because God will bless you. If you walk carefully along the narrow path and make the most of your time and opportunity, God will pour out His blessings upon you. In a sense you're redeeming the time for yourself. Redeem the time—use it in a way that will give God glory.

Every day brings new opportunities to be seized for God —opportunities for good, for righteousness, and for holiness. Galatians 6:10 says, "As we have, therefore, opportunity, let us do good unto all men, especially unto them who are of the household of faith." In other words, we're to grab every opportunity we're given.

84

Some people always intend to pray, study the Bible, and tell their neighbors about Christ—but they never get around to it. The greatest fool in the world is the fool who wastes time, who spends opportunity without a return.

Have you been telling the Lord for years that you're going to spend some time with Him? Have you done it, or have you let opportunity after opportunity go by—never redeeming the time? Use your time effectively. Grasp every opportunity you can. Don't be lulled to sleep by our fat society.

Holding a Piece of Eternity

Here's a statement to think about: Opportunity is in respect to time what time is in respect to eternity. The only piece of eternity you'll ever hold in your hands is the opportunity of this moment. You can't live in the past, you can't live in the future—you can live only in the present. We hold an opportunity in our hands, and it's the only piece of eternity we'll ever hold. I can hold eternity in my hand when I maximize each moment.

D. Squandering Opportunity

There are many biblical texts that warn people of their limited amount of time to apply divine principles.

1. "And the Lord shut him in" (Gen. 7:16). When Noah and his family were in the ark, God shut the door, and it was too late. Opportunity for others was lost.

2. "And the door was shut" (Matt. 25:10). The five foolish virgins had unprepared lamps when the bridegroom came, so the door was shut and the marriage feast went on without them.

3. "The night cometh, when no man can work" (John 9:4).

4. "Ye shall seek me, and shall die in your sins: where I go ye cannot come" (John 8:21).

5. "I will come unto thee quickly, and will remove thy lampstand" (Rev. 2:5).

6. "O Jerusalem . . . how often would I have gathered thy children together . . . and ye would not!" (Luke 13:34).

Time after time, year after year, century after century, God called out to Israel; but they were a stiff-necked and hardened people who wouldn't listen. God's heart was broken, and their opportunity was lost.

The greatest case of lost opportunity was Judas Iscariot. He spent three years with the Son of God, yet he walked away, hanged himself, and was dashed to pieces on the rocks below (Matt. 27:5; Acts 1:18). What a wasted opportunity!

When are you going to study the Bible? When are you going to teach? When are you going to pray? When are you going to tell others about Christ? When are you going to minister to others with your spiritual gift? You had better do it while you still have time—before it's too late. Don't waste your opportunity.

Paul says in Romans 13:11-13, "And that, knowing the time, that now it is high time to awake out of sleep; for now is our salvation nearer than when we believed. The night is far spent, the day is at hand; let us, therefore, cast off the works of darkness, and let us put on the armor of light. Let us walk honestly, as in the day; not in reveling [wild parties] and drunkenness, not in immorality and wantonness [shamelessness], not in strife and envying." In other words, we have only a limited amount of time. And we need to live according to God's principles within that time frame.

I would call a man a fool who threw away jewels or money, but I would call him a bigger fool if he threw away an hour. There's a world to be won, a church to be built, and a God to be glorified. There's no time for meaningless activity!

The believer who walks in wisdom knows his life principles and his limited privileges.

III. THE LORD'S PURPOSES (v. 17)

"Wherefore, be ye not unwise but understanding what the will of the Lord is."

We are to have a sense of urgency, but not so much that we panic, because then we're useless, frantically running all over the place. Verse 17 is a rock we can plant our feet on.

It's one thing to have a sense of urgency, but it needs to be channeled into God's will for our lives. We can't run off half-cocked, doing all sorts of activities. It's critical that our limited privileges be prescribed by the Lord's purposes. We don't need more activity or a proliferation of more busybodies. What we need are people who are out teaching the Word of God and winning people to Jesus Christ. We could probably do without a lot of the other activities.

People in a mad rush don't get anything done, but people with a resolute determination to follow God's plan will get a lot done. Don't be unwise. A fool functions apart from God's will and runs off to do his own thing. It's important to find out what God's will is and then do it with a sense of urgency.

How Can a Christian Know the Will of God for His Life?

Since we know that God has a will for our lives, He must want us to know what it is. Therefore, we can expect Him to communicate it to us in the most obvious way—through the Bible, His revelation to mankind. The will of God is, in fact, explicitly revealed to us in the pages of Scripture.

God's will is that we be:

1. Saved—"This is good and acceptable in the sight of God, our Savior, who will have all men to be saved, and to come unto the knowledge of the truth" (1 Tim. 2:3-4; cf. 2 Pet. 3:9).

2. Spirit-filled—"Wherefore, be ye not unwise but understanding what the will of the Lord is. And be not drunk with wine, in which is excess but be filled with the Spirit" (Eph. 5:17-18).

3. Sanctified—"This is the will of God, even your sanctification" (1 Thess. 4:3).

4. Submissive—"Submit yourselves to every ordinance of man for the Lord's sake, whether it be to the king, as supreme, or unto governors, as unto them that are sent by him for the punishment of evildoers, and for the praise of them that do well. For so is the will of God" (1 Pet. 2:13-15).

5. Suffering for His sake—"It is better, if the will of God be so, that ye suffer for well-doing than for evil-doing" (1 Pet. 3:17).

6. Saying thanks—"In everything give thanks; for this is the will of God in Christ Jesus concerning you" (1 Thess. 5:18).

You may say, "These are good principles, but they don't tell me where I ought to go to school or who I should marry." But if you're saved, Spirit-filled, sanctified, submissive, suffering, and saying thanks, you can do whatever you want! That's what the psalmist meant when he said, "Delight thyself also in the Lord, and he shall give thee the desires of thine heart" (Ps. 37:4). If you're fulfilling those six principles, you're delighting in the Lord. And if you're delighting in the Lord, He'll give you the desires of your heart. Does that mean He fulfills the desire? Yes, but before He fulfills it He puts it in your heart. If you are living a godly life, He will give you the right desires—and then fulfill them.

When you know God's will, are mindful of your limited time and opportunites, and obey, you are going to make a difference.

Jesus is the perfect illustration of Ephesians 5:15-17. He always operated by divine principles (John 5:19-20), He was always aware of His limited amount of time (John 9:4), and He always functioned according to the Lord's purposes (John 4:34). He had a sense of principle: He always walked the righteous path. He had a sense of timing: He knew His course and grabbed every opportunity yet was never in a hurry. He was determined but was flexible and available for the most sensitive situations. And what a sense of purpose He had: He acted only in accordance with His Father's will—one step at a time. He's our pattern. If you're going to walk in wisdom, that is how you do it.

Focusing on the Facts

1. What does Job 14:14 indicate about the time each believer has on earth (see p. 77)?
2. What makes it difficult to walk in wisdom in the world (see p. 80)?
3. What does the Greek word translated "time" in verse 16 imply about the kind of time we are to redeem (see p. 80)?
4. Why does Paul connect the truth of walking wisely with redeeming the time (see p. 81)?
5. Why is it important that believers walk wisely and redeem the time (Eph. 5:16; see p. 82)?
6. Why does God give us opportunities to do good (see p. 82)?
7. How did Paul characterize the evil in Ephesus (see p. 83)?
8. What eventually happened to the church at Ephesus (Rev. 2:4-5; see pp. 83-84)?
9. How do we know that the world isn't going to become any better (see p. 84)?
10. Explain what Paul meant by saying we're to be "redeeming the time" (see p. 84).
11. Cite some passages that warn us of our limited amount of time to apply divine principles to our lives (see pp. 85-86).
12. Who is the greatest example of lost opportunity? Why (see p. 86)?
13. Where does the believer need to channel his sense of urgency in the Christian life (Eph. 5:17; see p. 87)?
14. Explain what God's will is for every believer (see pp. 87-88).
15. How can a believer know God's specific will for his life (see p. 88)?
16. Who is a perfect illustration of Ephesians 5:15-17? Why (see p. 88)?

Pondering the Principles

1. Review the list of sins that characterized Ephesus (see p. 83). Which of those sins tend to influence you today? Confess them to God and determine to repent of them. As much as possible avoid any further exposure to such sins. To help you do so, ask the Lord to give you opportunities to glorify Him in the midst of the evil around you. And when God gives you those opportuni-

ties, grab them. Don't let them pass while you're trying to decide what to do.

2. Review the section on how to know the will of God (see pp. 87-88). If you have wanted to know God's will for your life, you now have a biblical basis. Analyze your obedience to God in the six commands listed. Are you fulfilling God's will in each of those areas? Before you can follow the Lord's leading, you will need to be committed to Him in those areas first. As you commit yourself to following them, God will manifest His will through your desires.

Scripture Index

Topical Index

Moody Press, a ministry of the Moody Bible Institute, is designed for education, evangelization, and edification. If we may assist you in knowing
more about Christ and the Christian life, please write us without obliga-
tion: Moody Press, c/o MLM, Chicago, Illinois 60610.